THE CHURCH

THE CHURCH

BY

WOLFHART PANNENBERG

Translated by
Keith Crim

THE WESTMINSTER PRESS
Philadelphia

Translated from Part II of the German
Ethik und Ekklesiologie
© Vandenhoeck & Ruprecht, Göttingen, 1977

This translation Copyright © 1983 Keith Crim

Book Design by Alice Derr

Published by The Westminster Press®
Philadelphia, Pennsylvania

PRINTED IN THE UNITED STATES OF AMERICA
9 8 7 6 5 4 3 2 1

Library of Congress Cataloging in Publication Data

Pannenberg, Wolfhart, 1928–
    The Church.

    Translation of: Beiträge zur Ekklesiologie, pt. 2
of Ethik und Ekklesiologie.
    Includes bibliographical references.
    CONTENTS: Churchless Christians—The unity of the
Church—What significance does their common past have
for today's separated churches?—The significance of
eschatology for an understanding of the apostolicity
and catholicity of the Church—[etc.]
    1. Church—Addresses, essays, lectures. I. Title.
BV600.2.P34513 1983   262   82-23768
ISBN 0-664-24460-2 (pbk.)

Contents

PUBLISHER'S NOTE

The contributions to the study of the church presented here in original translations were previously published by Vandenhoeck & Ruprecht of Göttingen in 1977 as the second part of the author's *Ethik und Ekklesiologie*.

1
Churchless Christians

From time to time Christians are shocked by reports in the secular press about the decline in church attendance, reports that seem to indicate that Christianity is going downhill in our society. Only 15 percent of West German Protestants regularly attend Sunday worship, and at present in the major cities only 25 percent of the Catholics go to church every Sunday. Such reports lend encouragement to those voices which consider that the status of our churches as national churches, supported by taxes and administering infant baptism, is unjustifiable. They demand that the churches become voluntary organizations, to which only truly committed Christians would belong. Such demands overlook the fact that the 75 to 85 percent of Christians who do not attend church regularly still have their children baptized and confirmed, plan church weddings, and expect Christian burial, as well as bear the burden of paying their church taxes. Nothing warrants our assuming that these Christians are inwardly alienated from Christianity. Although there may be individual cases of such alienation, not even formal withdrawal from church membership necessarily means a rejection of Christianity. Several years ago Trutz Rendtorff, in his defense of "Christianity outside the church" (1969), rightly rejected the tendency to belittle as "Christians by habit" those who have moved away from the church's life. Even the piety of regular churchgoers can be merely habit, connected with a certain narrow-mindedness and self-righteousness, which is certainly not more Christian than the attitude of many who have distanced themselves from the church. Christians who have reservations about the life of the church are often more open and less pretentious about what it means to be a Christian than active church members are. Often they are merely repelled by the religiosity of church members who are doing what they think is stylish. In many cases a change in pastors is enough to awaken a nominal Christian's interest in the church.

Are the ways in which Christians express their distance from the church entirely new in the history of Christianity? Such is the assumption of those alarmists who regard the decline in church attendance as a sign of the approaching end of the Christian religion. But at least since the fourth century, when Christianity became a mass religion, there have been varying degrees of commitment to the life and work of the church. In the Middle Ages, with the separation between clergy and laity, there developed in several stages a lay culture which maintained a greater or lesser distance from the church. Nonetheless "Christianity outside the church," in the dimensions that are familiar to us today, is, beyond dispute, a product of the modern age. And this specifically modern form of a churchless Christianity cannot simply be regarded as having continuity with earlier experiences of the Christian laity. It is closely connected with the splintering of medieval Christianity into mutually exclusive, mutually condemnatory denominations. In particular, as a result of the bloody religious wars in the Netherlands, France, Germany, and England between 1550 and 1650, many persons were unable to regard as believable the exclusive claims of the opposing denominations that each embodied the Church of Christ. During the Thirty Years' War, Friedrich von Logau wrote:

> If Christ's way to change the world
> Had been to persecute and kill,
> Why, then *he* would have crucified
> Those Jews who sought to do him ill.

Another of his satirical poems goes:

> Lutheran, Popish, Calvinist—
> These three creeds their views propound

But our doubts must still remain—
Where can Christendom be found?

The ruthless conduct of the religious wars discredited the churches, but even the fact that each belligerent party believed it had an exclusive claim to absolute truth and communion with God was enough to discredit them all. The largely indecisive outcome of the wars of religion produced a permanent situation in which the churches held a questionable position, and skepticism concerning their militant exclusivism was by no means necessarily based on a total rejection of Christianity. Clearly the denominational quarrels did severe damage to the credibility of Christianity in modern times.

As a consequence of the indecisive outcome of the wars of religion, political and social life has had to find a new basis that was undamaged by sectarian conflicts. This development had its start in countries where more than one denomination existed, but over the next centuries it led throughout Europe and America to the autonomy of political, economic, and social life over against religion. Religious allegiance likewise became more and more a private matter. The various churches, separated as they were from each other, lost their claims to universality. On the other hand, society and culture remained permeated in a general way by Christianity. Even the new, religiously neutral public realm still had to base its legitimacy on Christian principles. Thus, out of the Reformation emphasis on Christian freedom there came the demand for tolerance and religious liberty, and, as a result, the demand for general civil liberty. The modern formulations of human rights developed (under the pressure of the lessons of history) out of the idea of Christian liberty, of freedom from sin as the result of faith in Christ. The development of the idea that this had general applicability to all humanity as the foundation of a new, nonsectarian, common basis for life in society was itself dependent at the start of the modern period on legitimation in terms of the principles of the Christian tradition. But this expression of Christianity with its claim to universal validity in the form of a free, tolerant, and at the same time socially responsible Christianity could no longer find appropriate expression in the churches and their sectarian struggles.

In this manner the denominational divisions led in the modern world to a "Christianity outside the church." This development was intensified in Protestantism by the reaction in the churches against the rationalistic Enlightenment of the eighteenth century. In Germany in the nineteenth century the neo-pietistic awakening became dominant, so that from then on many Christians who did not share the pietistic spirit came to regard the piety that reigned in the churches as narrow and strange. In Catholic regions, for other reasons, especially the disputes over the hierarchical understanding of episcopacy, there were similar developments, which in contemporary times have become widespread.

In the perspective of this "Christianity outside the church," open to the world, but with reservations about the church and in part alienated from it, the churches place too much emphasis on questions of doctrine, especially those doctrines which distinguish the churches from each other. Yet this Christianity outside the church is dependent on the churches for its continued existence. There are various reasons for this, two of which I want to consider here. First, it is dependent on the churches for the transmitting of Christianity, and second, it is dependent on them in dealing with the frontiers of life.

1. The churches transmit through their instructions, their theology, and their proclamation that fundamental knowledge of Christianity without which even the Christians outside the church could not preserve their consciousness of belonging to Christendom. Even these Christians, in spite of their distance from church life, must depend on the churches precisely because the churches, by their teachings, preserve and pass on the awareness of that which is distinctive to and essential for Christian faith. It is possible to be personally in disagreement at one point or another with the form in which the knowledge of what is Christian is handed on, or to emphasize or modify it for one's own use, in order to adapt it to one's own interpretation or current experience. But even such individual adaptations and emphases are possible only on the presupposition that the Christian faith is transmitted in the churches. Private Bible-reading is not adequate for this purpose, quite apart from

the question of the extent to which we can count on independent Bible study as an element in our general education.

The bringing together of the contents of the faith through the
teaching activity of the church is indispensable as preparation
for Bible-reading, as the object of discussions on the basis of
one's own study of the Bible, and often even as the only way in
which Christian knowledge is transmitted.

Thus Christianity outside the church remains dependent on
the teachings of the church, which it rightly or wrongly
criticizes. It must remain so if it is concerned with preserving
its Christian identity, especially so far as the next generation is
concerned. It is the misfortune of this modern form of Christianity—open, tolerant, and freedom-loving—that it has found
no institutional form of its own but must depend for its survival
on the denominational churches. This is the case even though
for contemporary Christians these churches, in their denominational form and because of the particularism of their sectarian features, are unable to lay any claim to general validity as
institutional expressions of Christianity.

But when even so the denominations claim such universality
for their specific form of Christianity, they cannot avoid falling
back into sectarian bias, and there is nothing that makes the
churches less trustworthy than narrow denominationalism and
fanatic exclusivism. Many Christians—and in recent decades
their numbers seem to have grown significantly—want to be
considered Christians first and only secondly Protestants or
Catholics, in the sense of the Roman Catholic Church. Such
Christians more or less preserve their loyalty to the denomination in which they grew up, but without unreservedly accepting it as the universally valid institutional form of Christianity,
the claim the denominations make for themselves, at least in
the sense found in their own tradition. The churches, for their
part, cannot avoid the question of the universal validity of the
Christian message and the Christian faith. Just as the message
of Jesus cannot be understood without the claim to finality
which he asserted, so too the Christian faith is inconceivable
without the claim to be universally valid for all.

Since the time of the apostle Paul the Christian mission has
moved forward on the assumption that the Christian message

is universally true and valid, and from its beginnings Christian theology has taken as its theme the universal validity of the Christian tradition. At the same time the way the content of the Christian faith is formulated has changed again and again. Indeed, it had to change in order to make clear, in terms that can be understood in each new age and each changing perception of reality, that which is valid for all humankind in the Christian message and in Christian doctrine. But today the denominations with their creeds no longer represent the universal reality and truth of Christianity. Since the Reformation they have become, as they were called then, "religious parties," merely specific forms of presenting Christian truth, forms that are destructive of each other's credibility. Thus the Christian outside the church, in his familiarity with the contemporary world, can in his individual case be closer to the universality of Christianity, which unites in itself all the truth of reality—that is, to true catholicity—than are church members, especially those who confuse a narrow denominational outlook with the total truth of Christianity. We might cite such examples as the narrow piety of those who stress only sin and repentance, or the equally narrow-minded belief in the formal authority of certain church offices and office-bearers, especially when the positions taken by those officials are so obviously partisan and irrelevant. Even so, those Christians who feel loyalty to the universal human truth of Christianity, as they understand it, and for that reason have serious reservations about the denomination from which they have come, must look to those denominations because the public exposition and transmission of Christianity, which nourish the faith of individual Christians, have today no other form than that of the denominations.

In this ambivalent relationship to denominational Christianity, the Christian who is primarily interested in the universal truth of the Christian faith and less in its denominational distinctions has, in reality, an ally in theology, at least insofar as theology is not mere partisan propaganda for existing authoritarian positions, but with unrestrained criticism and self-criticism concerns itself with the question of the validity of the Christian tradition for all humanity. Because this understanding demands a high degree of complexity in theological language, the possibility unfortunately is slight that nonspecialists will be able to recognize how and to what degree theology involves their own concerns, specifically the concern for that which is of universal validity in Christianity. In addition, Christian theology, despite all its efforts to emphasize the universal truth of the Christian tradition, is tied to denominational Christianity, because to this day no better institutional form for the fellowship of Christians has been found than that provided by the denominational churches.

Institutional Church

2. These last observations lead to the second and deeper reason why the Christian faith, even the faith of Christians outside the church, cannot exist totally without the church. Christian faith needs a community as the context for its life, and only in such a community can it develop. This is illustrated with fullest clarity by the origin of Christianity in the religion of Israel. The God of Israel is a God who wills that there be justice and peace in the shared life of people in community. That is why he chose individuals for the sake of choosing a people and chose a people for the sake of all mankind. To make real the lordship of this God through peace and justice among his people would be the expression of the social destiny of humanity—the realization of the common salvation of all persons through this one people. For all mankind to live together in peace and righteousness has been, throughout political history, the unfulfilled destiny of men and women as social beings, and this would make it possible for each individual to attain integrity and wholeness, to achieve success.

Church as community

Church as servant of world

The social nature of faith in Israel's God (who is also the God of Jesus) and the universal validity of that faith are closely related. When Jesus proclaimed that God's Kingdom was at hand, he was speaking of the God of peace and social justice and was saying that the center for all true righteousness is that love which brings forgiveness and human solidarity. Jesus' message that the Kingdom was at hand led inevitably to the formation of a community of those who through their unity with Jesus and his message attain a new unity with one another. And this community is an expression of God's destiny

Church as Sacrament

for mankind. The Christian church demonstrates this principle in its celebration of Jesus' last supper with his disciples, where the fellowship of each individual Christian with Christ becomes the basis for the solidarity of all Christians with one another. Moreover, our unity with Christ demands and provides the basis for a solidarity with all men and women, because the God of Jesus is the one God of us all. For this reason the Christian church has, since its origin, understood itself as a community which in its life together already represents for all persons that life in the spirit of love, peace, and justice, which contains within it the promise of the consummation of human community. To put it differently, the Christian community in its life together makes visible the lordship of God, which is the future of the world, the future of all mankind. The idea of God's lordship is not an optional addendum to the idea that the destiny of human society is life together in peace and justice. On the contrary, the biblical and Christian awareness of God's lordship is the sole condition for peace and righteousness among men and women. Where people govern, the rights of the governed are continually being violated, and peace is shattered. It is only there where, instead of all human rule, God himself rules, that peace and justice can flourish unhindered in human communities. Therefore the community of Christians is based on the unity of each with Jesus Christ, who declared that God's lordship is the decisive criterion for the success or failure of each human life, and who thereby declared the lordship of this God as the extension of the sway of his forgiving love.

Since its beginnings then, the Christian church has believed that its fellowship already represents the future community of all persons in the Kingdom of God, where the human longing for peace and justice is to find its fulfillment. But what do we see when we look at the church? Not only do we find human lordship exercised by bishops, and church presidents, and pastors, where God alone should reign. All too often the spirit of love and justice is missing as well, and so too is any tangible expression of community. People sit side by side in the same pew without knowing each other. The real expressions of human life in community are found outside the church where *[handwritten annotations in top margin: "Sign and Instrument of 1) intimate union with God + 2) of the unity of the whole human genus L.G. 1, 5"]*

people work or play or live their family life. At best the churches express symbolically in their liturgy the community of Christians as the "sign and instrument of human unity," as it was so beautifully stated at the Second Vatican Council and at the Assembly of the World Council of Churches in Uppsala in 1968. Of course they preach the message of reconciliation, and in a still somewhat one-sided manner call for solidarity with distant nations, but these denominational churches do not show any capability of being reconciled with each other, of annulling their centuries-old condemnations of one another, or of recognizing each other as partial churches, parts of the one church of Christ, and of seeking together for ways to express more clearly in their own life and work the one community based on the love of Christ.

This situation makes it difficult for any alert Christians—not only those outside the church—to identify with these churches or to recognize in them a sign that the community of the Kingdom of God is a realm of love and peace, of freedom and joy. Our separate churches are more concerned with preserving their "denominational heritage," defending the customs of speech and piety they have clung to through the centuries and maintaining their present offices and institutions, than they are with taking seriously the necessity of a reformation, their transformation into the "sign and instrument of human unity," through God and Christ. *[handwritten margin note: "Criticism of The Church"]*

Perhaps the reason we have so many "Christians outside the church" is that it is so hard to identify with these separate churches in all their complacency and immobility. Thus the relevance of the Christian faith may easily come to depend on a community of life reestablished on the hope for the coming of the Kingdom of God and of Christ. The Christian outside the church is like the Christian in the church who feels uncomfortable in those pious circles which have the answers to everything, whether it is a question of the correct life of faith or the organization of the congregation's life. Such Christians are likely to see themselves restricted to a more or less individualistic Christianity. Christianity of this sort is found everywhere today and often involves a consciousness that something is lacking, a longing for a more convincing form of Christian community that could not be separated from the life shared with those out in the world. But when this lack and this need find no fulfillment in the existing forms of Christian community, then resignation may set in. This leads to individualistic Christianity outside the church, but does not necessarily produce a comfortable feeling. The Christians in the church differ from the so-called loners probably only in still being able to find and experience those symbols of the fellowship in the Kingdom of God through the love of Christ. Even though that fellowship may no longer be expressed in the total life of the church, church members can perhaps still experience its symbolic presence in worship. Aside from that, their Christianity is often every bit as individualistic as that of the Christians outside the church. And vice versa, the Christians who seldom or never take part in the regular worship of the church might still feel in those high points and turning points of life that they are involved in a larger, common context of meaning. At birth and death, at the passage from childhood to an intellectually independent existence, and at marriage, Christians who otherwise consider themselves outside the church search for a symbolic union with a life that is grounded in God.

The responsible officials of the churches customarily regard with sorrow or disapproval the distance or even alienation of so many members of their churches from church life. But nothing will be accomplished by mere exhortations to attend church faithfully. Those who by virtue of their office are responsible for the form and organization of church life must seek to discover the reasons Christians get along without the church, beginning with a look at the deficiencies in the performance of their own duties. Ultimately they are the ones responsible for the form of the churches and for the realization, in the churches, of the one Church of Christ. Anxious expectancy and a lack of imagination concerning the renewal of the church are no excuse for neglecting needed reforms. But neither does a zeal for reform of all sorts of secondary matters constitute an excuse for neglecting the real, central reform of the church in terms of its original destiny, of which we are again and again made aware in our own day, that is, to be the symbol and implement of the unity of mankind, not the symbol and implement of human lordship, but of human community in peace and righteousness, which is based on God, and which can indeed have no other basis.

This understanding of the nature of the church leads directly to three conclusions, which are also demands for a reform of the churches, and for which not only church officials are responsible but also all individual Christians.

(1.) The model of human community which the Christian church is to represent dare not be indebted to human lordship for its unity, but only to the lordship of God himself. This unity must not rest on the spiritual lordship of bishops, and certainly not on the bureaucratic lordship of holders of official positions in the church. Of course the community of Christians, like every human community, needs an office that is responsible *Pope,* for its unity on the basis of a common faith. In the Christian *Bishops,* church this office has found its classic expression in the office *Pastors* of the bishop, and such an office in the service of Christian unity through a shared faith is necessary at all levels of church life—at the local level, at the regional level, and also at the level of the whole of Christendom. Without such an office, organized and structured at different levels according to areas of responsibility, the unity of all Christians is not fully realizable, and the community of Christians cannot become the "symbol and instrument of human unity." But in actuality these offices and responsibilities have again and again been exercised in the form of a lordship of office-bearers over other Christians, instead of serving the lordship of God in contrast to all human lordship. Wherever a church leader relies on the authority of his office in order to compensate for the inability of his decisions and pronouncements to convince anyone, there is the possibility that service under the lordship of God may be perverted into human lordship. This holds true for the position of the pastor in his local congregation just as much as it does for the pope of the Catholic Church in his responsibilities for the whole church. The formal authority of each office must therefore be more closely and effectively connected with the process of forming judgments in the congregations and throughout the whole of Christendom than is the case today.

This must be done in all the churches, not only in the Roman Catholic Church.

(2) Only if the community of the church is based solely on the lordship of God and of Christ can the church be the symbol and instrument of the unity of mankind. Only belief in the lordship of God as exemplified in the work of Christ can bring about a free human community characterized by peace and justice. The church cannot be true to this task by supporting purely political movements, whose goal is merely an exchange of one human authority for another, by which peace and righteousness among mankind are not furthered.

(3.) The church can have only symbolic significance for the destiny of mankind to participate fully in a community of peace and justice in the Kingdom of God. It cannot by itself achieve this unity in a world where relationships rest on the lordship of some men and women over others, because in all the forms of human community the common interests of all are protected by a few individuals and must often be asserted in opposition to all other individuals. Not all the changes in the form of government or the order of society can affect this fundamental reality. Even the Christian church itself, although it does not constitute any political community, always faces the danger that its offices will be transformed into instruments of spiritual lordship over men and women. As an instrument for achieving the unity of mankind the church can function only through activities that are expressions of the symbolic nature of its existence as a sign of that unity. It is this which constitutes the sacramental nature of the church's life in the meaning of the traditional Augustinian definition of sacrament. Just as the church's contribution to the unity of mankind is dependent on its existence as a sign of that unity, so too the symbolic representation of the nature of the church through worship is of central significance for the essence and life of the church itself.

(4) For this reason the Lord's Supper, which is a visible and concentrated expression of the essence of the church, must be rediscovered as the center of the church's worship so that this worship may regain its symbolic function as a sign of the nature of the church and as the expression of the church's

mission to strive toward a realization of the unity of mankind. The Protestant churches, especially in Germany, must become aware that the symbolic function of the church as a whole and of its worship in particular has become impoverished and obscured at this point, because the celebration of the Lord's Supper has not been central to the church's worship.

The church's understanding of itself as symbol and instrument of human unity demands a reformation of Christian teachings and Christian doctrine. It is by no means obvious that the teachings of the church are prerequisites for the true realization of the unity of mankind under the lordship of God and for the functioning of Christian community in this task. A reformulation of Christian doctrine in this direction is not the task of theologians alone. It would be appropriate also for the official documents of the church to express the possible contribution of the Christian faith—and also of the Christian community of faith—toward solving the problems of our own day, and to express this more clearly and convincingly than is usually done in the traditional formulations of doctrine in the church. Such a new formulation of Christian doctrine could also make it possible for the church finally to overcome the denominational conflicts that result from the creeds that have come down from the past. In the ecumenical discussions of theology in recent years it has been demonstrated again and again that the disputes which once raged over the most varied themes are no longer significant enough to divide the churches. In terms of the basic issues of our faith in Christ they are no longer particularly significant. Such negative conclusions, however, need to be supplemented by a new common formulation of the essential content of the Christian faith. Only then would the disputes over the faith be finally overcome. A starting point in this process can be found in the analogous statements concerning the nature of the church issued by the Second Vatican Council and by the Assembly of the World Council of Churches in Uppsala in 1968.

Overcoming the doctrinal divisions of Christianity is the indispensable condition if the church is to become a sign of the unity of mankind. Only by overcoming the conflicts among the denominations can there be a convincing realization of that

which the Second Vatican Council and the World Council
agreed is the nature of the church. Even today, of course, this
nature of the church is not entirely invisible. But there are
distortions, and the universality, the true catholicity of the
church, is obscured among us by the divisions and the mutual
denunciations of Christians against one another, as well as by
our inability to achieve reconciliation and to overcome these
conflicts that have come to us from the past. This is Christianity's most important task in our century. Any other reforms of
the life of the church will remain ineffectual unless this
problem is solved, unless the separated Christians mutually
recognize one another and express this recognition in the
common celebration of the Lord's Supper.

The modern phenomenon of Christianity outside the church
is, as we have maintained, primarily the result of the fact that
the churches of the separated denominations with their mutually exclusive claims to embody the one church of Christ have
lost their credibility. They can regain credibility only by
resolving the denominational conflicts, and by the mutual
recognition that each is a partial church of the one church of
Christ. This would not of course solve all the questions
involved in the problems of helping individual Christians
identify with the church. Nevertheless, the more our divided
Christendom succeeds, on all levels of human life, in presenting itself as the sign and symbol, and therefore the instrument,
of human unity, the less will individual Christians, whose
feeling of belonging to the church depends on the church's
universal relevance, feel a need to remain outside the church.
For the world in which we live is in need of at least the
symbolic presence of a deeply rooted solidarity that includes
all mankind and that is based on something more than the
totality of ecumenical concerns and interests or political
systems and their shibboleths.

2
The Unity of the Church:
A Reality of Our Faith
and an Ecumenical Goal

The ecumenical movement of our century arose out of a quickened awareness that the divisions which exist among Christians are intolerable. This was felt with especial urgency in the mission field, where the churches of the West transmitted their own divisions to other peoples and to the young churches arising among them, peoples who had had no connection with the sad and guilt-laden history of the West. Out of this experience came a powerful impulse toward Christian unity through dialogue and cooperation among the divided churches. This does not mean that Christian unity was merely the goal of well-intentioned human efforts. It was, rather, that in the face of all disappointments these efforts were the expression of new confidence and new strength, especially the strength to be patient despite the slowness of progress toward unity. That confidence and that strength were based upon the assurance that in Jesus Christ the unity of all Christians was already a reality. Through their faith in the one Lord and through their shared participation in him in baptism and the Lord's Supper all Christians already are united. Insofar as each Christian has a share in Christ, each also is bound to all other Christians in the unity of the body of Christ. This is true also of our faith, if indeed faith truly unites the believer with Christ, as is affirmed in the Lutheran understanding of faith as a commitment in trust which establishes one's security outside oneself in Jesus Christ. That holds true also for the one baptism, through which all Christians are united with Christ by his death and so share in the hope of participating in his resurrection life. The unity of all Christians in Christ is seen with greatest clarity, however, in the sacrament of the Lord's Supper, the Eucharist. The Second Vatican Council, in its Decree on Ecumenism, rightly said that the Eucharist both witnesses to and works toward the unity of the church.

Therefore, prior to all human efforts, unity already exists because Christians are Christians, because, that is, of their "union" with Jesus Christ. This Christian unity, founded on and existing through Christ, is nothing other than that fellowship which we Christians repeatedly acknowledge in worship through the Apostles' Creed and the Nicene Creed, confessing the one holy, universal, and apostolic church. Consequently the efforts of the ecumenical movements are directed toward the reunion of Christians, not in the sense of a return to the historical state of Christianity before the divisions arose, but something much more urgent, a reunion in the sense of turning to that unity which already exists in our Christian faith and is one of its constituent elements. *Unitatis Redintegratio* (the Latin title of the Decree on Ecumenism) requires repentance and a turning to Jesus Christ himself.

In the light of that unity already given through Jesus Christ, the fact of Christian divisions can only be judged as an expression of failure, a straying from the path, which casts doubt on the Christian identity of each individual Christian and refutes the claim of any of the separated churches to be the church of Christ. The alienation of so many men and women from the church in the course of modern history, the extensive secularization of public and, to a large extent, private life—all this must be regarded as the concrete result of the loss of credibility which the denominations suffer because of their rejection of one other as each claims to be the one church of Christ. That modern secularism expresses itself in alienation from Christianity is not a fate that has come upon the churches through outside factors. It is the consequence of their own sins against unity, the consequence of the church divisions of the sixteenth century and of the inconclusive religious wars of the sixteenth and seventeenth centuries, which left the inhabitants of territories embracing more than one denomination with no choice but to reconstruct their life in community on a common basis unaffected by sectarian differences. The historical experience of a progressive falling away from the church and even from Christianity itself ought to be regarded by the churches as a call to repentance. When the apostle Paul asked the Corinthians in reference to their quarrels, "Is Christ divided?" (I Cor. 1:13), he was so convinced of the impossibility of such a situation that the question needed no answer. Christ cannot be divided. How shocked Paul would be by the fragmentation of Christianity into churches that reject one another. And how dumbfounded he would be by the complacency of Christians and their official leaders. They have been living for centuries with this situation without being disturbed by it or at least being challenged by the historical consequences of these divisions to feel that God himself is questioning their obstinacy and complacency.

It is no solution to say that the unity of Christians in the one church is expressed by the invisible reality of faith, hidden in this evil world, as though unaffected by our divisions. The thesis of the invisibility of the church contains an element of truth only when the awareness of a greater, more comprehensive unity in Christ, a unity that goes beyond the present reality of the church, becomes the incentive to make this greater unity visible. At New Delhi in 1961 the World Council of Churches expressed this by declaring that the unseen unity now hidden in Jesus Christ must be made visible in every place through all Christians being led by the Holy Spirit into a fully committed community. That this has not happened must be considered an expression of lack of faith and as resistance to the working of the Holy Spirit. How weak would any faith be that could rest content with an invisible unity of those who believe in Christ. Unfortunately the thesis of the invisibility of the one church has often led to such complacency and has been misused to justify Christian sloth and indifference in the face of a divided Christendom. Need I add that the confession of the visibility of the church can also be misused to justify a smug and complacent attitude? This happens when one part of the church lays unrestricted and exclusive claim to be absolutely identical with the church of faith. This form of self-justification has been found on every hand throughout the history of a divided Christendom.

One of the high points of authentic Christian spirituality at the Second Vatican Council was the confession of the guilt of all churches, including the Roman Catholic Church itself, for the divisions in Christianity (Decree on Ecumenism II.7) and in this connection the acknowledgment (though with reservations) of a limiting of the expression of the church's own catholicity, and of the forms in which it is expressed, as a result of the fact of Christian disunity (ibid., I.4). Unfortunately the common guilt of all the churches for their own existing divisions did not receive a similar official and formal acknowledgment from the responsible Protestant church officials. And in the document of the Roman Catholic Conference of July 1973 on the Mystery of the Church (*Mysterium Ecclesiae*) one searches in vain for the insights of the Council, which are fundamental to the cause of Christian unity. All Christian churches must join in confessing their shared guilt for Christian disunity, as well as their responsibility for its consequences. Only through such confession of guilt can the power for repentance be found. And conversely, a confession remains ineffective if repentance is not then translated into action. Anyone who is serious about repentance will not be content to let time slip by without taking action.

From church officials on both sides we heard recently that we should not try to rush the movement toward Christian unity, and that, moreover, in a very short time a great deal has been accomplished. Both of these statements are true. The cause of Christian unity would certainly not be served by a new sloughing off of groups who are not as far along on the road to greater understanding among Christians as others think they ought to be. And unless we are thankful for the progress already made in mutual understanding and in working at common tasks, all that has been achieved so far could be endangered. Such factors, however, are no justification for a pause in ecumenical development, an artificial slowing down of the process of cooperation and understanding. Protestant church leaders should remind themselves daily that the rise of Protestant denominations is not the result of the success of the

Reformation, but an expression of its failure, and that the Reformers were striving for nothing less than the reform of the whole of Christianity. The leaders of all Christian churches should become more fully aware that they bear a special responsibility for the unity of all Christians and not only for the members of their own denominational communities.

Today, when so-called "ecumenical enthusiasm" is regarded with calm reserve, and when the reunion of all Christians is thought of as a goal whose realization still requires more time, it is often the case that the seriousness of the consequences of Christian disunity for the identity of one's own church is underestimated. The unity of all Christians is not some optional feature of the nature of the church, which is desirable, but can, if necessary, be dispensed with. According to the doctrine of the early church, unity, along with apostolicity and catholicity, is essential to the existence and the nature of the community of the church which is sacred to its Lord. This means that the being of the church itself is in question if its unity is not realized. How can the church be—as it is called in the phraseology of the Second Vatican Council and of the 1968 Assembly of the World Council of Churches in Uppsala—a "sign and instrument of the unity of mankind," if it is splintered into mutually exclusive church communities? The claim to be the church of Jesus Christ is highly questionable when voiced by the separated churches and their officials. This problem is more pressing now than ever before, because the separate churches today regard the members of the various other churches as Christians. Centuries ago when today's divided churches hurled their verdicts of damnation against each other (verdicts which even now have not been formally revoked), each church could at least still regard itself as the only true church of Christ, from which the heretics had separated themselves. Today, even according to official Catholic doctrine, the situation is different. Even those Christians who are separated from Rome are regarded as followers of Christ and members of his body. This raises the question of whether it is not essential to the identity of the church as the church of Christ that all his followers be brought together in its fellowship. Is the church as understood in the ancient creeds fully realized as long as not all Christians are united with it? The Second Vatican Council, in the Dogmatic Constitution on the Church (I.8) and also in the Decree on Ecumenism (I.4), declared that the one church of Christ "subsists" in the Roman Catholic Church. This wording is clearly more reserved than that of earlier statements of the Roman Catholic Church about its ecclesiastical identity. By not making exclusive claims, it seems to leave the way open to the possibility of reaching understanding with other churches and of supplementing its life by the "elements of truth" which they have preserved (*Lumen Gentium* 1.8), and at the same time to the possibility of a more complete realization of the unity and catholicity of the Roman Catholic Church itself. In *Mysterium Ecclesiae* (1973), the formula that the one Church of Christ subsists in the Catholic Church is brought into play against the concept that the one Church of Christ does not yet have any visible existence, that it is totally invisible and must be brought to visibility. But in each of the present denominational churches the visibility of the Church of Christ has been realized only in very broken form, as long as none of the churches unites in itself all those whom it itself recognizes as disciples of Christ. In this situation the degree of the visibility of the Church of Christ in the present-day denominations is dependent, among other things, on their openness to a greater and more comprehensive realization of the catholicity of the church in a community which included all Christians and in which the mutually exclusive denominational churches could become partial churches in a more comprehensive, truly Catholic Church. Protestants can therefore agree to a Vatican formula of the subsistence of the one Church of Christ in the Catholic Church of today, because this formula in the documents of the Council does not seem to assert an exclusive claim to full identity. To be sure, Protestants will add that the one Church of Christ also subsists in the other churches of our day, even though these churches may differ in the degree to which they have preserved and made real in themselves the elements of the saving mysteries of Christ. Can the Catholic Church also agree to such a thesis of a manifold subsistence of the one Church of Christ in today's separated churches? Even for Protestants this can be done only by going beyond the exclusivism and narrowness of the original Protestant concept of the church, whose criterion for legitimacy was the purity of the doctrine taught, purity in terms of the Protestant theology of the Scripture. Without the thesis of a manifold subsistence of the Church of Christ in the separated churches of our day, even though there is variety in the degree of completeness of that subsistence, we would be left with an exclusive claim for a single specific church, one among the many, which would still have to gather into itself the elements of truth that have strayed away. But such a picture does not fit the ecumenical situation of the separated churches in our day. Only by their mutual recognition of one another will it be possible to attain a more complete realization of the unity and catholicity of the Church of Jesus Christ, through which the rich Christian heritage of the modern Roman Catholic Church, with its doctrines, its life of worship, and its institutional form, could bear fruit in a new way for all of Christianity.

Therefore we should affirm the visibility of the one Church of Christ in today's separated denominations, even though that visibility is fragmented. It will vary according to the degree of the completeness and purity with which the saving mysteries of Christ have been preserved and expressed. In any case, the visibility of the saving mysteries of Christ and his church can be found only where there is a living concern for the greater unity of all Christians, for where such concern is lacking, the church becomes a sect, a schismatic group that has separated itself from the totality of the body of Christ. This is why it is so shocking that leading church officials give the impression through their statements that there is plenty of time to see about the unity of the church. Anyone who in his position as officer of the Church of Christ makes such statements raises doubts about his authority. At all levels of church life, the officers of the church bear a responsibility for its unity.

The true legitimation for the office of bishop in the church may well lie in the fact that this office is the classic expression of the office responsible for the unity of the church. This involves concern for the unity between the believers entrusted to him and the apostolic tradition, and on the basis of this tradition, with one another as well. It also includes the unity of the bishop's own community with all other Christian communities in the unity of the same apostolic faith. The central significance of the office of bishop for the church does not depend on any proof of historic continuity with the time of the apostles. It is well known that significant historical difficulties in the second century stand in the way of such proof. But from the beginnings of Christianity, the task of preserving the unity of Christians in the apostolic faith, and thus in Jesus Christ himself, has been of greatest importance, and the establishment of the office of bishop in the church has far-reaching legitimation as the classic expression of the institutional aspect of this task. This is at least implicitly recognized by the Protestant churches, although the task of proclamation and the administration of the sacraments are in the foreground in the description of church authority in the Protestant confessions. The tasks of teaching the doctrine purely and of rightly administering the sacraments always include the task of preserving the members of the community in this one apostolic doctrine and in the unity of the mysteries of Christ. The task of preserving Christian unity has in the office of bishop a functional correspondence to the founding of the unity of the church through Jesus Christ himself. This unity, however, is realized appropriately only when the concern for community with Christ (whether on a local, subregional, or regional level) involves all Christians, that is, involves the unity of that community with the fullness of the apostolic heritage and with the whole of Christendom. Thus an office in the church, at whatever level, involves a concern for the unity of all Christians; this is the conciliar aspect of the office of bishop. Therefore in the present situation of the church each office-bearer in one of the separated churches should also be aware of a shared responsibility for those Christians who are in other churches. A continuous shared concern for the positive contributions and the special point of view of those Christians outside one's own church could give to the decisions, the statements, and the actions of each office-bearer of our separated churches a form of (conciliar) Catholicism that is rare today. Such continual concern for those who are separated from one's own church is especially to be desired in the bearer of an office which regards itself as the highest permanent office, with responsibility of all Christians everywhere.

The desirability or even necessity of such a supreme office can best be approached in ecumenical discussions by recognizing the role that the responsibility for preserving Christian unity plays in defining the nature of church offices. It is my opinion that one of the most important contributions of the disputed and much misunderstood Memorandum on Church Offices issued by the University Ecumenical Institutes in the spring of 1973 is that it gave a central place to this understanding of church offices and by doing so opened the way to a consideration of the significance which the office of bishop and the papacy have for the church. The cause of Christian unity will be advanced if we perceive that it requires a permanent office responsible for unity at all levels of the church's life—at the local and the subregional level, but also at the regional level and at the level of all Christianity. The whole Christian world needs an office that is especially concerned for Christian unity and that under certain circumstances is authorized to speak and to act in the name of all Christians.

Our generation saw how much this can mean for Christians far beyond the bounds of the Roman Catholic Church through the charismatic figure of Pope John XXIII, who was, in many situations, the spokesman for all Christians. But, we must ask, how can the charismatic actions of this one man be included in the institutional form of a supreme office that would be responsible for the unity of all Christians?

Today Protestants, and all other Christians separated from Rome, do not have such an office concerned for Christian unity. The Protestant churches must be made more aware than they are at present that what they lack is, as the Second Vatican Council rightly noted, essential to the unity of Christ's church. It is therefore necessary to achieve greater clarity about the distinctive nature of church offices in general and about their significance for the unity of the church. Article 7 of the Augsburg Confession says that it is sufficient (*satis est*) to the unity of the church that there be unity in understanding the gospel and in administering the sacraments. In view of the responsibility of church officers for Christian unity, which is affirmed even in the Protestant confessions, this statement must be expanded. In addition, it is necessary that at every level of the church there be offices that are responsible for the unity of all Christians. And if such an office is necessary at all levels of the church's life, then it is necessary at the level of the whole of Christianity.

The Roman Catholic Church, as is well known, affirms that such an office already exists, in personal union with that of the bishop of Rome. If we once acknowledge the desirability and necessity of a permanent office that at the level of all Christianity is responsible for the unity of all Christians, we cannot arbitrarily reject that claim. Protestant sensitivities concerning the papacy, which in the light of historical experiences are quite understandable, should not stand permanently in the way of an objective consideration of the claims of the bishop of Rome. It seems to be more conducive to progress to take this claim at face value. If there already exists in the office of bishop of Rome a special example of responsibility for the unity of all of Christianity, should not the union of the separated churches be the first and most urgent concern of the pope? In all his pronouncements and decisions, should he not take account of the difficulties and problems, as well as of the possible positive contributions of those Christians separated from Rome, instead of merely being concerned with preserving the faith of the apostles in that church, and among its members, which in the present day calls itself Catholic? It would be significant, perhaps decisive, for the cause of Christian unity if at every opportunity it were made clear, openly and publicly, that the pope was concerned with the cause of all Christians, especially those who are today separated from Rome, and if he were to make visible in all his actions the community in Christ which binds all Christians together. In the degree to which the bishop of Rome went beyond the present boundaries of the Roman Catholic Church and included in his thinking and decisions the problems, concerns, and possible contributions of the other churches to the life of contemporary Christianity, giving all this clear expression, in that degree his claim to be the representative of all Christianity could gain credibility outside the Roman Catholic Church of today. The example of John XXIII shows what possibilities actually lie open in this direction.

In the first place, recognizing the positive contribution of other churches must mean providing a place for their distinctive features within an enlarged Catholic self-understanding. In the same way, these other churches should rediscover and make their own the riches of the Catholic tradition, such as the central significance of the Lord's Supper for worship, and of the office of bishop for the form of the church's community. On both sides much remains to be done, but much has already taken place since the Second Vatican Council, especially in regard to the basic concerns of the life of the congregation, but also in theological dialogue.

Second, the urgency of the cause of Christian unity demands that the Roman Catholic Church and those churches separated from Rome undertake official negotiations toward the goal of affirming the things we already have in common. They should also investigate whether and under what conditions it is possible to recognize each other as churches of Christ and to revoke the mutual anathemas from earlier centuries that are still in effect today, and that in any case continue to affect the relationships of the churches to one another. During the past decade the theological discussions which the Second Vatican Council desired and encouraged have made so much progress in dealing with the doctrinal disagreements still remaining that the ground has been prepared to a large extent for official negotiations among the leaders of the churches. Such negotiations are indispensable if definitive progress is to be made toward overcoming the divisions that exist among Christians. The initiative, however, must come from the bishop of Rome, and by such an initiative the pope would express in a form ⌐relevant to today's conditions the claim that his office has universal relevance for the unity of all Christians. A significant step in preparation for an offer to engage in official negotiations would be for the Roman Catholic Church to state the assumptions and conditions for recognition of the churches separated from Rome, for it can hardly be expected that these churches would abandon their distinctive historical nature and simply adopt the present dogmatic, liturgical, and organizational form of the Roman Catholic Church. If it can be assumed that everyone knows that a reunion of all Christians cannot come about by such means, then we must ask under what assumptions and conditions the Roman Catholic Church might see itself able to take appropriate steps. At this point ecumenical discussions are stumbling in the dark.

Third, in official negotiations of the churches it would be necessary to clarify the form that the unity of the church of Christ might take in the future in the relations of the churches to one another. This involves not merely the shared fellowship of the Lord's Supper, which presupposes the mutual recognition of church officers. It requires, in addition, the establishment of appropriate bases for cooperation among church officials at the local, subregional, and regional levels. And finally it demands progress toward an agreement on the question of an office responsible for the whole of Christianity. The starting point for such an agreement could be a new application of the distinction between the pope's responsibilities as patriarch of the Latin church and his universal episcopal authority for the whole of Christianity, as has been suggested in various theological presentations in recent years. The responsibility of the pope for the present-day Roman Catholic Church could thus be distinguished from his responsibility for all Christians, and the form and conditions of this responsibility would have to be the subject of negotiations among the churches.

Fourth, such negotiations could be the preparation for a new ecumenical council, in which the Protestant and the Orthodox churches would participate on a equal basis. Only a council can clarify the bases of a new "corporate" (Bishop Tenhumberg's term) unity of Christian churches in a form that could be binding on all churches. The prayers of all Christians should be directed toward the convoking of such a council. In the meantime, the various churches, still separated from one another, have the opportunity of making their own organization, their worship, and their faith so rich, and so to strengthen their unity with Christ, the one Lord of all Christians, that in their own life they would become capable of participating in a council, become capable, that is, of coming together in such a council in the fellowship of the Holy Spirit.

3
What Significance
Does Their Common Past Have
for Today's Separated Churches?

Concern for the unity of the church cannot be limited to the situation in which we find ourselves today. The task of understanding today's separated churches demands both an understanding of future tasks and an understanding of the divisions that brought about the present fragmentation of the Christian church. In the past history of today's churches lie the causes that led to these divisions. Can we discover in that past history sources of strength for overcoming our present separation? We cannot simply assume that this is the case. While it is undeniable that a long common heritage preceded today's divisions, still that unity may be something which we cannot regain, because in the periods of separation there arose new questions which led to divisions, and today it is simply no longer possible to return to the time before those questions were raised.

Be that as it may, every Christian church has occasion for making its appeal to the church of the early Christian centuries. The reason for doing this is not so much that the early church was undivided. Even though most of the divisions that exist today had not yet arisen, there were still in those early centuries numerous divisions which cast doubt on the idealized picture of the early church as undivided. It is not necessary to idealize the early church in order to be interested in it. Our interest is motivated by our concern for the Christian identity of today's churches. Are these churches still identical with the Christian church as it existed from the time of the apostles? Without such historical continuity it is impossible for a Christian church of our day to understand itself as a community of faith that resulted from the missionary work of the apostles. The question of the unity of the church involves not only the relationship of today's churches to one another but also, and perhaps foremost, the relationship of each of today's churches to the origins of Christianity and to the history that resulted from those origins. Especially when the churches of today appeal to their apostolic origins and to the early Christian church, the contrasts among them become glaring, because each of them understands itself as the authentic continuation in the present day of those Christian origins and sees in the other churches deviations from those roots and from their expression in the early church. Thus the relationship of the separated churches to their common history immediately takes on the nature of a quarrel over the heritage of early Christianity.

This can be illustrated by the relationship of the Reformers and the churches of the Reformation to the early church and especially to the early councils and confessional statements. Luther felt that no teaching of the church was necessarily free from error, and that he could evaluate even the church fathers and the early councils of the church by the standard of his own knowledge of the gospel. He was, however, of the opinion that *de facto* the three early confessions, especially the Apostles' Creed, were appropriate brief summaries of the gospel, and he regarded the doctrinal statements of Nicaea and Chalcedon as formulations of the "exalted expressions of the divine majesty," which are not "in doubt or dispute," as he wrote in 1537 in the Schmalkald Articles (*WA* 50, 197f.). Luther believed that the doctrine of "our redemption," which in his day was in dispute, was not merely a supplement to those doctrines of the early church but that they, especially the doctrine of the two natures of Christ, were the key to the doctrine of justification and could even become for him "the most forceful expression of the doctrine of the cross and justification."[1] At first Melanchthon regarded the relationship as less close, but in the first article of the Augsburg Confession of 1530 he appealed to the Nicene Creed as the basis of the Lutheran doctrine of God, and in the third article he appealed to the Apostles' Creed in support of the Christological statements of the Augsburg Confession. In terms of imperial law this appeal was of the greatest significance for the Protestants, because by making it they placed themselves firmly on the basis of catholic faith and thus were not in violation of the early church laws against heresy. From 1539 on, Melanchthon placed even more stress on the meaning of the three ancient confessions and the first four councils. In 1545 he wrote in the so-called "Wittenberg Reformation" (a document prepared for negotiations with the Church of Rome) that the doctrine of the Augsburg Confession was "in agreement with the Apostles' Creed and the Nicene Creed, with the ancient holy councils, and with the positions of the first pure churches" (*Corpus Reformatorum*, Vol. 5, col. 582). Similar expressions are found in the statutes of the University of Wittenberg of 1546. Around this same time, Calvin, in the second edition of his *Institutes of the Christian Religion* (1543), also expressly affirmed the dogmas of the first four ecumenical councils.

For Melanchthon as for Calvin, the agreement of the early church with the teachings of the gospel assumed basic significance as a guide for understanding Scripture.[2] The doctrinal consensus of the early church became, along with the Scripture itself, a supplementary criterion of contemporary church teachings and a standard for the exegesis of Scripture, under the assumption that this consensus among the early Christians did not include anything except the teachings of Scripture. For Melanchthon, the only churches of his day that corresponded to this earlier and purer church (he was thinking only of the Latin churches of the West) were those which accepted Luther's teachings (*Corpus Reformatorum*, Vol. 28, col. 369). Melanchthon felt that in his day the one catholic church was found in visible form only in the Lutheran churches. The appeal to the early church had the function then of strengthening his conviction of his own orthodoxy and of bringing that of the other side into dispute. In the seventeenth century the Helmstedt theologian Georg Calixtus revived this perspective and gave it a new emphasis. He regarded the consensus of the early church and its correspondence with Lutheran doctrine as axiomatic, and at the same time he endeavored to find in that consensus of the first five centuries a basis for the unity of the Protestant churches with each other, and, in the more distant future, for union with Rome as well. Calixtus illustrates the way in which the polemical appeal to the early church could be transformed into an irenic appeal. But in this form it was the expression of an unhistorical romanticism, because it rested on the assumption that it was possible to return directly to an earlier phase of the history of the church. The factors that made this impossible and separated the present day from that idealized past were not taken into account. It is this which rendered such irenic romanticism illusory. Specifically, it ignored the fact that the early church of the idealized past also included the starting point for the medieval papacy, against which the Protestants were directing their polemics. This difficulty applies also to Melanchthon's appeal to the early church. While it was possible to bring against the medieval church the charge that the points in which it differed from its origin in the early church constituted departures from the life and faith of that church, it could not be denied that on the other hand the way had already been prepared in the early church for these changes.

This side of the matter was given prominence by the strict Lutherans of the sixteenth century, whose leading theologian was Flacius Illyricus. In the Magdeburg Centuries, Flacius, by applying the standards of the Scripture, found that as early as the third century there were departures from the apostolic origins of the church, that from the fourth century on they became more extensive, and that from the seventh century on they were dominant.[3] According to F. Christian Baur, Flacius demonstrates "how dominant the shadow side becomes in a history of the Christian church which regards the bishop of Rome as the embodiment of the Antichrist." We must not, however, lose sight of the fact that this view of church history inevitably came to dominate the perspective of the Reformation to the degree to which the church of the medieval papacy was understood as the result of a development whose beginnings were to be found in the early church and which was regarded by Flacius, using the standard of agreement with

Scripture, as a steadily increasing departure from that starting point.

The interpretation of the history of the church as a falling away from the truth was revived in the nineteenth century by Albrecht Ritschl and his school in new circumstances. The departure from the apostolic age was now no longer sought only in the formation of papal centralization but also in the Hellenization of the primitive gospel through bringing metaphysical ways of thinking and the heathen mystery religions into the early church. Adolf von Harnack, who gave this concept its classic formulation, saw the beginnings of the Hellenization of the gospel within primitive Christianity itself, and even in the writings of the apostle Paul. In his concept, early catholicism did not begin with the rise of the primacy of Rome, but with the monarchical episcopacy of the second century, as well as with the formation of the creeds and of the canon of Scripture as instruments of a dogmatic legalism foreign to the original gospel. The concept of church history as a falling away from the truth was carried so far by Harnack that this process was thought of as having begun in the midst of the primitive church itself. Thus the shared past of the separated Christian churches shrank to the question of a canon within the canon, and finally to Jesus himself.

The early Protestant position, as represented by Flacius, was that the age of the apostles and the New Testament canon was without exception the pure source of the Christian faith, the source which is common to all Christian churches prior to the falling away from the truth. Harnack felt, however, that the ambiguity of historical development permeated even this period of Christian origins, and that this was due to the same factors that had made it impossible to maintain the idealization of Christian antiquity in contrast to the medieval church. Just as the patristic age of necessity contained the seeds of the Middle Ages, so too historical investigation sought to discover the sources of early catholicism even in primitive Christianity itself. Therefore, as Ernst Käsemann has put it, the Scripture is the basis, not of the unity of the church, but of the multiplicity of denominations. Each denomination finds its own past in the Scripture. Although the Bible bears testimony to the common origin of all Christian churches, even in the writings of the early church the paths that led to the separated churches of a later time had already diverged from one another. There is also another reason why the Bible as a witness to the common origin of all Christian churches cannot be taken as the common denominator for the churches, that is, that the present-day life of all Christian churches has continued to move farther from the early church. The churches exist today in a world that is fundamentally different from Christian antiquity. They confront problems that were unknown in the period of Christian origins and for the most part confront them together. Therefore the question arises whether that which the churches have in common today is not to be discovered in the pressure of the tasks and problems shared by all the churches rather than in their common origin. The common origin says very little about the necessity and possibility of community in our present world.

A different picture could emerge only if the past which the separated churches share were also their future. This cannot be the case for either the apostolic age or the church of the early ecumenical councils. It is, however, the case for the person of Jesus of Nazareth, who is not only the historical starting point for all historical forms of the Christian faith but also the Lord who is coming again and who is the focus of our Christian hope. Because the one Jesus is not only the historical origin of the diverging lines of development in church history but also the one future of all Christians, yes, of all mankind, because of this and only this, there comes to us from the common past of the separated churches a compelling call for reunion. Because the destiny of Christians to share in the blessings resulting from the sovereignty of God is inseparable from their unity in Christ, the divisions that have arisen in the history of the churches testify to the guilt the churches have incurred by departing from the destiny determined for them. And since the mission of the apostles and the faith of the early church also point toward this future under Christ, our study of the statements of the Bible and of the decisions of the early church can be more than a retrospective view of a common heritage. These statements and these decisions can also be-

come signs pointing us to the future of Jesus Christ, to the
common future and destiny of the separated churches. Thus
the mission of the apostles and all subsequent Christian
missions have taken place in the light of God's future judgment
on the nations, when Christ returns as judge. In the light of this
future judgment the Christian faith is based on God's reconciling mankind to himself. The future of our returning Lord
becomes a time of salvation for all those who are now united
with him through faith, and thereby with one another in the
community of the church.

Therefore Christ's future makes the unity of Christians a
necessity. But this future will not be identical with a return to
the early years of the church or to the earliest forms of the
church's life. On the contrary, in the light of the problems that
all the churches confront today they must decide what is
demanded of them by God's future judgment and by the return
of the Lord as constituting the shared future of all Christians
and all churches. They must decide what changes they must
make in their present institutions in order to conform to God's
future. This is quite different from a romantic return to a past
that is deemed normative, whether that is the period of the
early church or of primitive Christianity. The price of such a
return to the past is an ignoring of the distinctive features and
tasks of each church's own historical situation, that is, of all
the features that cannot be made to conform to the idealized
epoch of a classical age. Ignoring the uniqueness of the present
and the tasks that it sets for us, however, brings us into conflict
with history. Where union was actually achieved by Protestant
denominations in the nineteenth and twentieth centuries, these
unions were not based, as Calixtus had hoped, on the consensus of the first five centuries but on the historical situation and
the changes it had brought, as the separated churches saw that
situation confronting them, and in the light of which their
traditional differences appeared less significant for their understanding of the faith.

Jesus Christ, as the common future of all Christians and of
their currently separated churches, is decisive for the question
of Christian unity. To be sure, this future under Christ is
secure for us only through his past history, through that

history's witness to the mission of the apostles, and through the faith of Christ's church for the future. But today the common past of all Christians can point the way to a new community and a new unity only to the degree to which we deal with the future of the church and the world in terms of that past. If this is done, then even the history of Christian divisions appears in a new light. Through the acknowledgment of our common future under one Lord, the separate histories of the churches must be accepted as our common past, while the particularism of denominational self-understanding will, by contrast, merely discover in what we have in common that which divides us. When Christians believe they are divided from one another in the fundamentals of the faith, community can only seem to be present, and can do no more than conceal deep-seated conflicts. The mistrust that results has often hindered theological conversation between the divided churches and prevented any real understanding. When, however, our future under Jesus Christ determines the unity of all Christians and their churches, we will be able to discern even in the divisions of the past and in the separate development of the various churches the common history of Christianity, however lacking, however guilt-ridden, however fragmented it may be. It is only when the history of those churches which are regarded as heretical is accepted as a part of one's own history that the appeal to our common past will be free from quarreling about which side is legitimately able to appeal to the early church and to the time of the apostles, and to feel that it is the genuine heir of that past. This quarrel over the heritage of the Christian beginnings will cease when we have found in the conflicts of church history, in the separate development of a fragmented Christianity, the unity provided by the crucified Christ, whose sufferings are prolonged by the fragmentation of the history of the church, fragmentation which can be over-come and reconciled only through faith in the future of the one risen Lord.

4
The Significance of Eschatology
for an Understanding
of the Apostolicity and Catholicity
of the Church

The designation of the church as "apostolic" is usually understood to mean that the church stands in a relationship to the apostles of Jesus Christ, a relationship that is the basis for its present existence as well as for its essence. All denominations regard the apostolic origin of the church as normative for their teachings and their structure. There are, however, profound differences in the way that the churches see the apostolic origin as a norm, and consequently in the answer given to the question of how the churches of the present day demonstrate that they are in harmony with their apostolic origin and thus make their apostolicity manifest. How can these differences be overcome by means of the common belief in the apostolic character of the church? Is it sufficient to go back to the time of the church's origins and seek to establish more conscientiously than ever before the normative significance of this apostolic age for the subsequent history of the church? Or would such a program contain within itself the difficulties that lead to a greater emphasis on the differences? I shall endeavor to show that the problems are insoluble if the apostolic period as such is accepted as the norm for later church history. I will also endeavor to show that on the other hand the concept of apostolicity contains an eschatological motif from the teachings and activities of the apostles which moved forward beyond their own age, leaving behind those features of the apostolic age which were conditioned by the times, and having significance as a guide for later generations, generations that were not at all in the range of vision of the early church but that find themselves on the road to that future toward which the work of the apostles was oriented.

Above all else, the church laid claim to continuity with the apostles in reference to their teachings, the tradition that they handed on. The beginnings of this are already found in the Pastoral Letters. But the church soon came to appeal to the apostles for legitimation of its pastoral office and the whole of its structure. Later the church traced its liturgy back to the apostles and also looked to them for the model of a truly Christian life, a *vita apostolica*. In the course of the history of the church this underwent a variety of interpretations.

Down to the second century, the various local churches had regarded it as obvious that in all that they did they were following the apostles and thus were sharing in the true faith, but then in their disputes with the Gnostics this belief came to be regarded as a claim that required a doctrinal basis and justification. Irenaeus was the first to provide such a basis and justification for the already existing consciousness of continuity with the apostles and their teaching. He accomplished this by drawing on the writings of the apostles to justify the doctrines that had been handed down in the churches and were now being disputed by the Gnostics. Irenaeus appealed to the power of the Holy Spirit sent by the risen Lord as the basis of the authority of the apostles (*Adv. haer.* III.1). In contrast to the appeal of the Gnostics, especially Marcion, to individual apostles and apostolic writings while rejecting others, Irenaeus stressed the unanimity of the apostles (*Adv. haer.* III.13.1) and thereby protected the unity of the teachings contained in their writings. And in contrast to the Gnostic appeal to special traditions not recorded in the apostolic writings, Irenaeus contended that the true tradition could be found only in the unbroken succession of bishops in the churches maintaining continuity with the apostles (III.3). Along with the episcopal succession, the priests of those churches had also received from the apostles "the sure charisma of the truth" (IV.26.2).

Thus the assertion of the Gnostics that "only those who understand the tradition are able to discover the truth of the Scriptures" (III.2) was not rejected. It could easily have been

rejected on the basis of Irenaeus' positions formulated elsewhere, that the teaching of the apostles was accessible "openly, reliably, and completely" in the Scriptures, just as it had
been given publicly (III.15.1). Instead, Irenaeus agreed with
the position that a tradition of the "living word" was necessary alongside the Scriptures to ensure that they were properly
understood. He wished to show that this tradition also is to be
found only in the apostolic churches. Tertullian stressed this
point of view even more strongly. In the writings of both,
tradition is in remarkable tension with concern to use the
apostolic writings to justify their positions in the controversy
with the Gnostics. The admission that the living voice of a
specific tradition was necessary to the understanding of the
Scripture inevitably created difficulties for the emphasis on the
Scripture as the criterion doctrine. Irenaeus and Tertullian
could avoid this problem only because for them it seemed
obvious that the church which was descended from the apostles formed a living unity with the apostolic writings which it
had handed down. It seems that in spite of changes in other
areas this remained axiomatic for the early and medieval
church. Only at the end of the Middle Ages did a change take
place. As a result of the priority that had been accorded to the
literal meaning of the Scripture for theological teaching since
the exegetical work of the Victorine school in the twelfth
century, methodological exegesis gained such importance for
the teachings of the various theological schools that a contradictory interpretation by the teaching office of the church
could be regarded as a denial of the truth.

There were isolated instances of such conflicts before Luther's day, but through him the conflict took on such basic
significance that it became necessary to decide which of the
apostolic principles that had previously been in harmony with
each other—the Scripture and the teaching office—should be
subordinated to the other. Both solutions created difficulties.
If the teaching office were accorded the final authority over the
meaning of Scripture, then the Scripture could no longer
function as an independent criterion for the apostolic nature of
the church's teaching tradition. In that case the agreement in
content between what is said by the contemporary teaching

office and the teachings of the apostles, as well as the apostolicity of the teaching office itself, would become questionable. On the other hand, the development from scholastic exegesis of the biblical writings "through themselves" (according to the principle "sacred scripture is its own interpreter") to historical-critical exegesis made clearer how great the historical distance is between the apostolic age and all later periods of church history, and not least the distance from the time of each specific interpreter of Scripture. Thus the question arose: how is apostolicity possible at all if it consists in agreement between the church of the present day and its historical origins? Does not the historical distance of the exegete from his text make the concept of apostolicity unusable as a norm because he lives in a world so different from the age of the apostles? The problem involves even the beginnings of Christian history, because the problem of apostolicity of the church belongs itself to a later age than that of the apostles. A historical approach is unable to identify in principle any agreement in doctrine between Paul and the Jerusalem apostles or among the various apostolic writings such as that which Irenaeus felt existed and regarded as basic to his concept of apostolicity. Neither can the attempts to trace the lists of bishops back to the apostles stand up under historical criticism, because it was only in the second century that the office of bishop seems to have established itself as the chief of the various early Christian offices. Such conclusions do not need to be absolute contradictions of the church's consciousness of its apostolicity, but they raise the urgent question of what—in the light of the differences between the apostolic age and all later periods of the church—is the basis of the connection with the apostles.

In an age that is aware of history, it is no longer adequate to point to the teachings of the apostles as if they were accessible in full agreement with each other in the New Testament and were applicable without modification to future periods. Neither is it adequate to contend that the apostles chose their successors in the pastoral and teaching office, because of the historical problems involved in the origin of episcopacy and the fact that succession in office cannot of itself guarantee continuing agreement between the holder of the office and its originator. Since the succession of ages is unavoidable, continuity with the apostles can be based only on a factor that is not limited by the distinctive features of the apostolic period but continues beyond the boundary of that age. The eschatological motif of the early Christian apostolate seems to constitute such a factor. A thorough discussion of this motif will lead us to a connection between apostolicity and catholicity. Finally, their common relationship to eschatology will cast light on the question of the degree to which both predicates of the church involve a confession of faith and cannot simply be established empirically.

I

It is presupposed in the usual understanding of apostolicity that the question is limited to the origin of the church and to the church's permanent connection with that origin. This view seems inadequate and in need of supplementation. It is generally recognized today that early Christianity was characterized by a remarkable eschatological consciousness, a consciousness of living in the presence of ultimate reality, which is still future for the world, but in Jesus Christ and thus in his church is already reality, though for the church it is reality only through faith in Christ and in the expectation of a future consummation. Should not this eschatological consciousness of the early church also find expression in the understanding of the apostolic office, so that it would be preserved in the concept of apostolicity? If the church calls itself apostolic not only in the sense that it was founded by the message of the apostles but also in the sense that it partakes of the spirit and mission of the apostles, and that in spite of the unrepeatable nature of the apostolate and the apostolic age it continues this mission through history, then the apostolicity of the church must include the essential motifs of the early Christian apostolate and provide for their continuance.

The early Christian apostolate was founded on the appearance of the risen Lord. This statement is based first of all on Paul, who knew that he had been called by the risen One to be his disciple (Gal. 1:12, 16; Rom. 1:5; I Cor. 15:10; 9:1). But Paul was also aware of a circle of "all apostles," which was not identical with the "Twelve." In this sense he termed the missionaries Andronicus and Junias "apostles" (Rom. 16:7). Even before the call of the apostle Paul this wider circle of "all apostles" must have been considered closed, since Paul had to characterize his own call to be an apostle as that of one "born abnormally late" (I Cor. 15:8, Phillips). If this circle of apostles is distinct from that of the Twelve, then its origin, or the apostolic office of its members, is most likely to be sought in the appearances of the risen Christ, as reported in I Cor. 15:7. The wider circle of apostles also included, according to Paul, the Twelve, or at least some of them (Gal. 1:17ff.). Paul probably regarded their apostolate also as based on the appearances of the risen Christ to them, although the Twelve had earlier been the disciples of Jesus while he was on earth, and although the number "twelve," which represents the twelve tribes of Israel, probably goes back to the time before Easter. The reference to an already existing circle of apostles shows that in affirming the connection between apostolate and a call issued by the risen Lord, Paul was sharing an already established early Christian understanding of the significance of apostleship. In the Gospels themselves the Twelve are at times termed apostles during the earthly ministry of Jesus (Mark 6:30; Matt. 10:2; Luke 6:13), but this can be explained naturally as a use in the pre-Easter situation of a title later applied to the same persons on the basis of their having witnessed the appearances of the risen Lord, a title that had become generally accepted. Only Luke states that Jesus had also called the Twelve "apostles" (Luke 6:13). This may be connected with a limiting of the concept of apostle to the circle of the Twelve (Acts 1:21ff.). Moreover, the Gospel tradition contains evidence of a special commission and sending forth of the disciples by the risen Lord (Matt. 28:16ff.). This agrees with the early Christian concept of the founding of the apostolate as found in the writings of Paul.

In the light of these data, theological reflection on the concept of the office of apostle and its significance must begin with the points of contact found in Paul's writings. What is involved here is not a mere private view held by Paul. At most, we find this in the defense of his own apostleship. In every other connection Paul's statements point to the original understanding of the distinctive nature and significance of the office of apostle in the early church, insofar as this can still be determined. Therefore theological discussion of what constitutes the office of apostle and the concept of apostleship in general must take its basic orientation from the meaning of the calling and sending forth of the apostles by the risen Lord. This does not mean that we must regard as irrelevant the Lukan concept of apostle, which has generally been in the foreground of theological discussions of the apostolate in all denominations. It can, however, no longer serve as the starting point of such discussions, but is to be considered a modification which it was natural for Luke to introduce on the basis of his (by no means unjustified) theological interest in the relationship of the early church to the pre-Easter ministry and teaching of Jesus. This Lukan interest can be affirmed by theology without necessarily adopting the Lukan restriction of the concept of apostle to the circle of the Twelve, which cannot be maintained on historical grounds.

What, then, can we learn about the nature of the apostolic office through its having been founded by the appearance of the risen Lord and his commission to those who saw him? Our starting point must be that which gives the resurrection appearances a meaning for the disciples different from that of the reality of Jesus before Easter. This is, first of all, the eschatological life from death which had now become reality in Jesus. Second, for this reason the post-resurrection reality of Jesus is the divine confirmation of the eschatological authority which Jesus had already claimed for himself before Easter. And therefore, in the third place, Jesus' appearing to the disciples meant for them a renewal of the mission for which he himself had given his life. The message that the power of the sovereign God was near at hand took on in this way new form in the proclamation that the lordship of God had become reality in Jesus himself, in his life and his fate, but above all through his resurrection from the dead. That the risen Christ called apostles and sent them forth is thus not something that was incidental to his resurrection appearances. Although not all those who were present at those appearances seem to have felt that they were called and sent forth (the five hundred brethren of I Cor. 15:6 are certainly not all to be included in the number of the apostles), and although the commissioning itself can be understood in various ways—as restricted to Israel or as including all nations—still the resurrection appearances do not constitute only the confirmation of Jesus' own mission but also the reaffirmation of that mission for his disciples.

The apostolate of the early church thus had its starting point in the experience of the eschatological reality of resurrection from the dead, as manifested in Jesus. But in addition, the mission of the apostles has eschatological significance. This is true especially of the mission to the Gentiles, which Paul, in the light of such eschatological prophecies as Isa. 11:10 (Rom. 15:12), understood as the fulfillment of the pilgrimage of the nations to Zion in the end time. In addition, the mission of the Jewish-Christian community to Israel also had eschatological significance. It called for repentance because of the imminent manifestation of God's lordship, as did the message of Jesus himself, but now it did so on the basis of the access to salvation which had already been provided by Jesus. The conversion of the Gentiles was regarded by such Jewish-Christian thought as a mighty act that had been brought about by God himself and that was to accompany the universal manifestation of his lordship (Joachim Jeremias). At this point the cross of Christ took on fundamental significance for Paul's understanding of the apostolate, because Paul saw the crucifixion as the rejection of Jesus by Israel for the sake of the law (Gal. 3:13ff.), so that from then on, God's appeal to the Gentiles was made without the law. The work of the apostle is thus not performed in the light of God's eschatological act in Jesus Christ: it points toward the goal of accomplishing the content of the eschatological promise itself, and it becomes itself the instrument of God's activity, preparing the way for the coming of the Kingdom. The present power of God's future lordship in the teaching and mission of Jesus finds its apostolic counterpart in the universal mission to all nations.

Thus the apostles are seen as continuing the eschatological

message of Jesus himself but in another form, in that Jesus himself had become the starting point and the content of his own message. It is precisely through this transformation of its form that the message remained the same. Jesus' message was that the power of God's lordship was determinative for the present age through Jesus' own life and work. It could be continued by his apostles only as the proclamation that ultimate reality had broken through in Jesus himself. The ultimate reality that was manifest in Jesus, however, was made effective for the present age by the world mission of the church. If the eschatological meaning of Jesus' message could remain the same for his disciples only by being changed, so it is also to be expected that the eschatological mission of the apostles could be continued by the churches which they established only by being changed, that is, only by including in their entirety their own historical differences from the apostles and the apostolic age in their understanding of the message of Christ as a message to the people of their own time.

II

At first glance it might seem that the church has not kept the eschatological aspect of the apostolic mission as a part of its awareness of its own apostolicity. While the mission of the apostles looked forward to the end of the world, which had already dawned with the resurrection of Jesus, the apostolicity of the church seems rather to involve a backward-looking orientation to the doctrine and work of the apostles. But this first impression needs clarification if a false posing of alternatives is not to distort the issue. It is possible that the church, by the way in which it looked back to the doctrine and work of the apostles, was expressing its consciousness of the ways in which it was different from the age of the apostles, and thus of the altered nature of its own apostolic mission. The church of the second century held firmly to the apostolic writings and was concerned to preserve continuity between its current life and its apostolic origins. By so doing, it was clearly expressing the finality, and thus the eschatological character of the message proclaimed by the apostles, because it was distin-

guishing the age in which it was living from the uniqueness of
the apostolic age, while at the same time recognizing that it
was the successor of the apostles, and was letting itself be
shaped by the eschatological mission which had been committed to it.

To be apostolic in the meaning of the eschatological mission
of the apostles is clearly more than merely conserving the
heritage of the apostolic doctrine. To be apostolic is to set
forth the finality, that is, the truth, of that which occurred in
the person of Jesus and was proclaimed by the apostles. In this
context, finality means the future truth of the world, which is
not yet brought to completion, that is, has not yet fulfilled its
essence. Therefore the apostolic doctrine is not expressed
through traditional formulations as such, but only through the
proclamation of the finality of the message and work of Jesus,
proclamation always related to the present day and always
casting light on present experience, as it sets forth the message
and work of Jesus as the truth that brings this unfulfilled world
toward fulfillment. When it does this, the universal mission of
the church is in one way or another a part of the apostolicity of
the church. In this sense the confession of the fourth century
to the full deity of Jesus, and that of the following century to
the unity of God and man in him, can be understood as
apostolic, even though the doctrine of the Trinity and the
Christological formulas and criteria of Chalcedon were clearly
far removed from the thought world of the apostolic age, and
cannot simply be derived from the New Testament writings.
The only thing that is essential to their apostolicity is that they
give clear expression to the unsurpassed, final truth of the
incarnation of Jesus Christ and do so in a way that is valid in
the language of their time.

Is it possible to understand the debates in the Western
church concerning the nature of grace, down to and including
the Reformation and Jansenism, in the context of the apostolic
interest in the finality of the person and work of Jesus Christ?
It cannot be denied that this motif was involved in the
formation of the doctrine of grace. For Augustine, human
dependence on God's grace meant dependence on Christ and
on his saving work, which mediates that grace. Thus for

Augustine it was an expression of the finality of Christ, not only for mankind but also for the life of each individual. In his opposition to the Pelagian concept of freedom, Augustine objected that if the salvation of the individual was determined through the individual's free choice to use the external help which was given through nature and the divine law, then Christ came into the world in vain. Similarly, Luther argued against the merit which was ascribed to the use of free will to supplement the working of grace. At issue therefore in a radical understanding of the doctrine of grace was the finality—or, as Luther said, the "honor"—of Christ. We can recognize here the apostolic spirit. The specific threats to the doctrine of grace should not be underestimated: that the concept of grace would become independent of the specific person and work of Christ, or that an exaggerated extrinsicality[4] of grace in relation to nature would obscure its proper theme, the inclusion of men and women in full salvation through Christ. The apostolicity of the doctrine of grace is revealed further in its specific tendency to include the individual history of each man and woman in their salvation through Christ. This produces a new understanding of the church as the distinctive community of grace through the incarnation of God in the one man Jesus. The doctrine of grace thus is true to the comprehensive aspect of the apostolic mission, expressed in the universal mission to all the world. Only through this comprehensive dynamic can the finality of Jesus Christ, the eschatological significance of his person and work, find full expression. The doctrine of grace, as applied to the individual, unfolds a third mark of true apostolicity, that is, that the saving truth concerning the world and mankind is not already apparent in the incompleteness of the present world, but only through its being transformed into that salvation which has already dawned in the resurrection of Jesus.

The above observations show that we cannot bring against the church the comprehensive charge that in the development of doctrine the eschatological orientation of the apostolic mission was lost. In reality, this apostolic motif has always remained active in the history of the church and in its teachings. In the teaching of the church the motif has been especially significant in the progressive doctrinal clarification of the finality of Jesus. This is its comprehensive dynamic, and, as represented in the resurrection of the One who was crucified, is its reconciling power. The express consciousness of the nature of the apostolic, however, did not develop to the same degree as did the activity in the church of the divine and apostolic spirit.

In the first place, in all denominations the theoretical consciousness of unity with apostolic origins meant a one-sided concern to find in the apostolic age norms and legitimation for the present life of the church, without paying much attention to the fact that the doctrines and life of early Christianity belong to an age long past. By regarding the apostolic age as the norm, the church lost its freedom to recognize which elements of its way of life and thought were limited and conditioned by the times. As early as the second century, there was a tendency to glorify the time of the church's origins, in clear contrast to Paul's understanding of that time, for Paul was fully aware of the distance between his own time and the eschatological culmination.

In the second place, the tensions and contrasts between the various New Testament writings (rediscovered only by historical research) and the disagreements which they expressed within the early church were ignored in the interests of the pious opinion that there was unanimity among the apostles. It was no longer seen, for example, that while the relationship of the apostle Paul to the Jerusalem church was marked by a concern for harmonious agreement, it was far from realizing such agreement. This all too harmonious picture of the early church must share the responsibility for the problem in the church, present since earliest times, that so little room would be granted for the development of conflicting opinions.

Third, the identification of what is apostolic with a way of life and thought that was long past brought with it the danger that because the church was seeking the norm for the present in the past, it would not be open to the new and distinctive tasks and opportunities of its own day, and the danger that the church would read contemporary issues into the biblical texts and endeavor to deal with the present as something foreign. In

all three points the desire for apostolicity, in the sense of a
normative function of the apostolic age with its thought world
and its ways of life, led the church to fail to see the historical
significance of the apostolic writings and to seek to validate
specific traditions and institutions as apostolic, in a way that
we would not consider legitimate today, that is, regarding them
as apostolic because they could be traced back to apostolic
practice.

In any case, it must be stressed, fourth, that this very lack of
historical reliability in the use of the designation "apostolic,"
and especially the unhistorical use of Scripture in periods
when the teaching and practice of the apostles were regarded
as normative, could have a positive function. Only in this way
could room be made for the new concerns and themes of each
age, and thus for the truly apostolic task, in the eschatological
meaning of the concept. In an age, however, in which we are
conscious of critical and historical issues, we can no longer
naively practice an unhistorical exegesis of Scripture or an
unhistorical use of the principle of apostolic origin, however
useful they may once have been. If we did, we would violate
our awareness of the truth and thereby damage the credibility
of Christianity, with its essential interest in true apostolicity,
the finality and comprehensive universality of the person and
work of Jesus.

In this age of historical consciousness, therefore, the church
needs a new concept of apostolicity that will allow it to
recognize without reservation the difference between the age
of the apostles and its own day, without thereby losing its
connection with the mission of the apostles. Attention to the
eschatological motif in the early Christian apostolate can help
us do this. The only criterion of apostolic teaching in this sense
is whether and to what degree it is able to set forth the final
truth and comprehensive universality of the person and work
of Christ in the transforming and saving significance of his
resurrection and its power that gives light to the world. To
demand that the teaching of the church be apostolic cannot
mean that everything that is known from the age of the
apostles should be normative for the present day, nor can it
mean that only that which is derived from the age of the

apostles can be regarded as valid today. It follows that the true *vita apostolica* is to be sought in the life of the church's leaders and in the life of individual Christians who let themselves be permeated by the final, all-encompassing, liberating, and transforming truth of Jesus. The *vita apostolica* does not mean copying the way of life of the apostolic age or what we think that way of life was, and it certainly cannot be lived by borrowing this or that form of life from the regulations of the apostles. That which was apostolic then may be irrelevant today or may even be a hinderance to our apostolic tasks. This insight enables the church to be free to live in its own historicity as opposed to that of the apostolic age and still remain in continuity with the mission of the apostles.

The relevance of the eschatological orientation of the concept of apostolicity can be made clear by our showing how it casts light on the critical and controversial interpretations of apostolicity in the churches of the Reformation and in the Roman Catholic Church. The Reformation churches regard the Scripture as the sole criterion of true apostolicity. The applicability of this criterion, however, became problematic in the course of the development from the Reformation principle of interpreting Scripture by Scripture to historical, critical research. Because of the historical distance between the present church and the early church, it is no longer possible to use the Scriptures of the New Testament to establish criteria for apostolic doctrine and apostolic life in the present day. As a result, the scriptural principle has led to the problems of hermeneutics, and these problems center in the question of the criterion for the recurring reformulation of the contents of the New Testament writings. Luther used the proclamation of Christ as such a criterion, and also as the criterion for apostolicity. Since the mission of the apostles was in fact a mission to proclaim Christ, Luther's criterion seems adequate, if proclamation of Christ is understood as interpretation of the universal meaning of the coming of Jesus and of the salvation which he brought. This was indeed, as said earlier, the goal and purpose of the mission of the apostles.

It seems to me that the Roman Catholic understanding of apostolicity also leads to a similar problem of criteria. In the

Catholic Church there is a further criterion of apostolicity in addition to Scripture and the confession of faith—the teaching and pastoral office of bishops and pope, with authority as successors of the apostles to interpret Scripture and the faith. It is not necessary for Protestants to reject this *a priori*. It involves the continuation of the apostolic mission in a changing world. The mission of the apostles developed a dynamic that reached far beyond the age of early Christianity and formed the basis of the continuing task of the church. The reason for this is that the mission of the apostles was directed not only to its own time but to the eschatological culmination and to the Last Judgment, that is, to the end of all human history. It was, of course, right to stress the uniqueness of the apostolic mission, in as much as it was based on the task directly committed to them by the risen Lord. But that by no means excludes the necessity of a continuation of this mission in the post-apostolic age. Since this mission founded the church as a whole, it is correct to point out that apostolic succession is primarily related to the entire community in the form of the various local churches and not exclusively to its leadership (E. Schlink). Nevertheless, it cannot be denied that any understanding of apostolicity in terms of the mission of the apostles is related in a special way to the task of providing leadership for the congregations in the light of this mission (even if it is provided through changed institutional forms), and to the continuation of the proclamation of the comprehensive and universal significance of the incarnation and earthly life of Jesus for the salvation of the whole world. The two tasks are intimately related, but that does not necessarily mean that the two functions must be united in the hands of one person. The question of the criterion for the continuation of the apostolic mission remains open, and the mere fact of succession can hardly be adequate. The concept of an unbroken succession in office beginning with the installation of successors by the apostles themselves is hard to defend on historic grounds, especially since interest in such a line of succession reaching back to the apostles cannot be documented much before the end of the second century. In addition, there is the vital question as to what guarantees that the successor will be true to the task of those who preceded him. Irenaeus himself referred in this connection to the charisma of office. But how can a charisma of office guarantee, not only for the holder of the office but also for the whole community which the office is to serve, that the occupant of the office will carry out his responsibilities? Reference to a charisma of office is not sufficient ground for an authoritative rejection of the question of whether the officer is faithful to his office. The only thing that helps is if the charisma of the office is understood in connection with the nature of the office itself, as it is determinative for the activity of the officer.

If, however, the charisma of the office belongs to the nature of the office, then there is the possibility of forming a public judgment as to that which faithfulness to that office requires in a given situation. Has the office-bearer acted in accordance with the leading of the charisma of the office or not? Has he acted or spoken in faithfulness to the office?

The only criterion for forming such a judgment is the distinctive nature of the office itself, insofar as it can be understood by someone who is not the office-bearer and thus does not possess the special charisma of the office, but has a share in the matter with which the office is concerned. Thus the criterion for forming an opinion concerning the faithfulness of officers of the church is the eschatological nature of the apostolic mission, which determines the necessity and also the direction in which this mission is continued beyond the age of the apostles. This provides, then, the basis for the institutional form which such a mission should take in order to accomplish its purpose in each historical situation of the whole church, that is, the specific organization of the one mission in a multiplicity of offices. The number of such offices, the division of labor among them, and the lines of authority do not always need to remain the same.

In addition to an institutional organization with various offices, the question of the church's mission in each situation involves also the decision which must be made in case after case for the sake of the mission of Christianity in the world. A criterion is needed for both these areas, and it is determined by the nature of the apostolic mission itself, in as much as it is a mission to proclaim Christ. This conclusion coincides with Luther's requirement that the proclamation of Christ be recognized as the criterion of what is apostolic. This cannot mean the application of an already complete Christological standard. Rather, the criterion of the proclamation of Christ points to the constantly new task of witnessing to all mankind in the most appropriate way concerning the meaning of Christ for universal and comprehensive salvation. This involves not only the teaching of the church but also the form which the church's life takes.

If we understand the apostolicity of the church in terms of the eschatological nature of the apostolic mission, we may find it possible to overcome authoritarian forms of the Christian tradition without sacrificing the role of the apostolic mission for the teaching and life of the church. These authoritarian forms have played a large role, not only in the understanding of church authority in the Roman Catholic Church but also in the understanding of Scripture in the churches of the Reformation (and in their concept of church offices too), and they claim legitimacy on the basis of the concept of apostolicity. The eschatological orientation of this concept seems to demand a new understanding of the offices of the church and to make such an understanding possible. These offices can be legitimated only by the apostolic mission. This provides for a flexibility in the form of the offices, in order to meet the demands of each new historical situation, but it does not interfere with the unity and (to the extent to which it is eschatologically oriented) infallibility (because of its finality) of the ongoing apostolic mission itself. On the contrary, it assumes them from the start, without implying that such unity and inerrancy must always be apparent in the performance of the office. The degree to which the structure, organization, and fidelity of the church's offices truly express the basic apostolic mission in its unity and inerrancy will of necessity remain the subject of discussion and criticism in relation to the task of such a mission, because the Spirit of Christ is bestowed on all Christians and because the redeeming truth of Christ should convince all mankind.

III

The universal scope of the apostolic mission, which is based on its eschatological nature, directly implies the idea of catholicity. If the eschatological mission of the apostles has found its necessary expression in its universal nature, then Christian communities can remain apostolic only under the condition that they understand that they are a part of the ongoing, universal mission and of its prior activities. Thus a Christian church can be apostolic only to the extent to which it is catholic.

Since the development of the concept of catholicity by Ignatius of Antioch and Polycarp of Smyrna in the second century, the emphasis on the catholic nature of the church and its life has been closely connected with the theme of Christian unity. In opposition to the appeal of the Gnostics to certain apostles and to the special transmission of truth which they were alleged to have begun, Irenaeus appealed to the agreement of all the apostles with one another. He also appealed to the agreement among themselves of the various churches of his day that could trace their origins to the apostles, as well as appealing especially to agreement with the Roman Church. He did not ascribe to it a monarchical position, but he did accord it a special rank in the circle of apostolic churches because of its large size, its age, the respect given it, and finally because it had been founded and led by the famous apostles Peter and Paul (*Adv. haer.* III. 5). While this argument did not use the later terminology, it did bring to bear against the heretics the catholic consensus, which immediately placed the heretics in the wrong, because they isolated themselves by dependence on a special tradition. As early as Tertullian the "catholic" rule of faith was explicitly contrasted with the special traditions of the heretics (*De Praescriptione haereticorum* 26).

In spite of the relationship between the unity of the church and its catholicity, the two attributes are not identical. The unity of the church primarily involves concern for the fellow-

ship of the already existing churches with one another. Catholicity, by contrast, goes beyond the limits of the existing
churches insofar as their present life still reveals elements of
particularities and narrowness when seen in terms of their
universal responsibility for mankind. The unity of the church is
an internal issue, both in reference to the relationship of the
various churches to each other and in reference to their unity
with the origin and norm of the Christian community and the
Christian faith. It also involves the unity of the individual
Christian with a specific community. The catholicity of the
church goes beyond this to include the church's relationship to
the world that is not yet permeated by the Christian faith. It is
not possible to speak of the catholicity or universality of the
church without taking into account the universality of the
salvation made known in Jesus Christ for all mankind and the
universal mission of the church to transmit to all the news of
this salvation and lead them to partake in it. The Second
Vatican Council emphasized anew that the apostolic responsibility of the church for the world is an element in its catholicity. But Cyril of Jerusalem had long ago specifically mentioned
this element in the concept of catholicity (*Catechetical Lec-
tures* 18.23), together with the church's geographical expansion and the realization of the fullness of the content of the
term "catholic."

The quantitative aspect of catholicity as the universal expansion of the church goes beyond the contemporary Christian
world and the past history of Christianity to include an aspect
that points toward the eschatological fulfillment of the church.
The catholic community of the church includes not only all
presently existing Christian groups but also those of its past,
back to the origins of Christianity, and those of the future,
down to the end of this world. Only in the glory of the
eschatological consummation will the church be fully and
completely catholic, since that consummation is not merely
the final stage of world history but also the consummation of
and judgment on all earlier epochs. Thus the catholicity of the
church is, in the strict sense, an eschatological concept. It is
not just that the *eschaton* is its goal, as is the case with the
apostolic mission; only in the eschatological glory will it attain

to full reality, which will include, among other things, the elimination of the contrast between church and secular society. This eschatological meaning of the concept "catholic church" does not mean that the church has no reality while it is on its way through history toward its eschatological consummation, but while the church is passing through history it can be only partially manifest as catholic. The simplest illustration of this is that each new epoch of the church's history is given form by only a few generations, and not by the earlier and later generations which also belong to the one community of the catholic church that endures through the ages.

The result of this is that in the ongoing, not yet fulfilled history of the church, catholicity is always tied to a single specific and therefore limited form of Christian life, in one or another Christian community, and also in the intellectual activity of individual Christians. In this history which is not yet completed, the fullness of catholicity is seen only in concrete, and as such, varied and specific forms. Seen then in this light, the view that catholicity demands uniformity in the life and order of the church, its liturgy, or its doctrine, is recognized as a misunderstanding. On the other hand, the opposite position, that the one true church remains invisible, is also wrong. It does not take into account that the fullness of catholicity is able to manifest itself under the special conditions of each specific situation. Of course none of these concrete forms of the Christian church is identical with the totality of catholicity. But it is possible for a specific church, stamped with its specific traditions and shaped by specific problems and tasks, to keep itself open to the fullness of the Christian tradition (including that of other traditions), to the multiple expressions of the contemporary reality of the Christian spirit, and to the fullness and newness of future possibilities and tasks for the whole of Christianity.

Where this takes place, individual churches and individual Christians can, in spite of the actual limits of their understanding and of their life, be representatives of the fullness of catholicity in the midst of history. But because each such manifestation of the catholic spirit remains specific and limited, and has not yet attained to eschatological fullness, no form which the one catholic church takes on can justify the claim that all churches must take on the same form. In the relationships of the various Christian groups to one another, catholic unity can only be expressed if they acknowledge and respect in one another the presence of the fullness of catholic truth in their specific modes of life, traditions, ordinances, and creeds. Individual groups, in their concrete limitations and commitments, look with hope toward the universality of the catholic truth, which will appear in the church triumphant at the eschatological consummation, but this does not assure any of them of a simple, handy standard by which they can acknowledge one another.

Yet the fullness of the completed church will display historical multiplicity caught up and reconciled in its glory, as step by step it comes to realization on the path of Christianity through history. Therefore each contemporary claim to catholicity must prove itself in three respects: first, through concern for continuity with the whole past history of Christianity and its heritage, especially the origins out of which the Christian faith draws its life; second, through a breadth which provides room for the manifold manifestations in which the Christian faith has been expressed in the past and in the present; third, through openness for new, future possibilities of Christian activity, especially in working toward the well-being of all mankind, those whose salvation is the goal of the mission of the church. These are criteria by which the churches can orient themselves in mutual recognition of the reality of a truly catholic spirit in the widely varying forms of Christian tradition and community. Identical forms of doctrine and church order are not prerequisites for this mutual recognition. It presupposes neither a *consensus de doctrina,* in the traditional Lutheran sense, nor identical organizational structure, but it can lead to the development of such common features. Even then, however, it would not be necessary to regard it as a failure if common formulations or institutions were interpreted differently and underwent different developments. Uniformity would destroy catholic multiplicity. Therefore we must not set arbitrary limits to the process of differentiation, to the development of differing and distinctive features. That would be a return to the demand for uniformly valid principles, even if such uniformity were limited to the defining of general boundaries. The life of the church must, rather, provide scope for the two tendencies—toward unity and toward differentiation—tendencies which in every society challenge and limit each other. The tendency toward differentiation functions in reaction to existing forms of life and thought that no longer appear adequate. The more this differentiation develops, the greater the need for a unity out of multiplicity, as long as no uniformity is imposed from outside.

The mutual relationship of the various regional or denominational traditions within the one Christian world should be thought of in terms of that type of multiplicity of concrete forms in which the catholic fullness of the church comes to expression. The multiplicity of such traditions in church order, doctrine, and liturgy does not exclude catholicity as long as each of them holds itself open, beyond its own distinctive features, for the Christian rights of the others and feels a responsibility, not just for its own tradition, but for the whole of Christian history and its heritage. In this process, certain expressions of the Christian tradition in history and in the present day can have especial significance for all Christians. Thus it is possible to accord a particular church and its traditions the foremost position within the whole Christian community. As Irenaeus said, such a position can be justified on the basis of age, size, or respect, but above all because of the demonstration of true apostolicity and catholicity. But no individual church, no individual manifestation of Christian catholicity can claim exclusive identity with the one catholic church, whose full appearing Christians expect at the future consummation, and in whose provisional manifestation they are now living in the variety of Christian communities. One consequence of the eschatological nature of catholicity is that no present manifestation, not even the highest, can lay claim to being catholic. None of them occupies the position of an absolute monarch in the total Christian world. Claims of that sort obscure the true catholicity of a church and distort its form through denominational narrowness and intolerance. The more clearly the true catholicity of a specific church and its tradition is expressed (for example, the Roman Catholic Church), the more gladly the community of the other churches will honor the actual preeminence of that church in the whole of Christianity and regard it as a sign and token of Christian unity. In this process, that specific church would have to remain conscious of the ways in which it differs from the catholic fullness of the consummated church, not only in its own order and doctrine but also in its relationship to the rest of Christianity. In the present day when the consummation has not yet been attained, eschatological catholicity can be manifest only on the condition that we do not confuse the always specific forms of its manifestation with the fullness of catholicity itself.

In this discussion it has been assumed that catholicity means not merely universality in time and space but a fullness of significance. This thought is based on the expectation of the eschatological consummation of the church, since that will bring together the variety of all that which is separated in time and space and transform it through participation in the fullness of God himself.

The idea of catholicity as the fullness of truth is especially relevant to the concept of catholic doctrine. But in this area also no historically concrete and thus limited form of the doctrine is identical with the whole truth. Therefore we must modify the saying of Vincent of Lérins that catholic doctrine is that which has been believed "everywhere, always, and by all." He took only the extensive and qualitative meaning of the word "catholic" as his basis and left out of consideration the aspect of fullness, especially as it is involved in the concept of eschatology. When we approach the question from an eschatological concept of catholicity, we must conclude that the fullness of Christian truth appears in each historical form of Christian doctrine but is never brought to full and complete expression. Thus it is always possible that the one truth of Christ can be expressed not only in a new way but also quite differently, even in opposition to earlier formulations of doctrine, without necessarily denying that these earlier formulations were in their time, even though limited, still an expression of the same truth of Christ. Even mutually opposed doctrinal statements such as those of the Council of Trent on the one hand and the Reformation creeds on the other—which in their own time stood in sharp opposition to each other—can be seen from a later point of view as both partially justified. And they can be recognized as expressions of the one truth of Christ, even though they were limited in their knowledge and in their legitimacy. This does not mean that they were necessarily mutually limited in relation to each other. In any case, from each new point of view the partial correctness of each doctrine must be capable of more precise expression in terms of the new understanding of the truth of Christ, because no forms that the one truth takes, not even provisional forms, should be lost to us. If we Christians do not yet have the whole truth, but must wait for it in the eschatological future, of which we experience here and now only a foretaste, then there can be genuine alterations of traditional doctrine without endangering the identity of the truth. True respect for tradition must always presuppose that even those who developed traditional doctrines remained oriented to God, who is always greater than any of their formulas. Only a Christian doctrine that mistook itself for eschatological truth would need to fear that a change of doctrine would inevitably also sacrifice the identity of the truth. The actual life, the actual history of all Christian churches, is in this respect richer than all previous, often astonishingly narrow understandings of the catholicity of its doctrine. Nowhere has only that been taught as catholic truth which was believed everywhere, always, and by all *in the same form*. The progress of doctrinal formulation has again and again corrected, not necessarily the faith, but the understanding of the faith, not as perceived only by earlier generations but also by contemporary church authorities.

This sheds light on the contrast between catholic doctrine and heresy. In an eschatologically oriented understanding of catholic truth a doctrine is not to be condemned as heretical merely because it departs from or contradicts an accepted or even solemnly proclaimed doctrinal norm. A teaching is heretical only when it ends in a partial truth, and there is unwillingness to include in it the fullness of the Christian heritage and the eschatological fullness of catholic truth.

All these considerations are implicitly intended to remind us what it means when we Christians confess that we believe one holy, catholic, and apostolic church. We are not merely affirming its existence. The catholicity of the church is an object of faith, because its catholic fullness will be completely realized only in the eschatological consummation. To be sure, it is beyond doubt that it is not just the future church that we confess as apostolic and catholic, but the present church as well. The present form of the apostolic mission has as the goal of its mission to mankind the task of bringing to new expression in each age the catholic fullness of the church. Thus the belief in the catholic and apostolic church becomes productive for the present day. It is only there where the apostolicity and catholicity of the church are understood as matters of faith and not as something that is easily verified that they both can be seen in the present life of the church as harbingers of the coming Kingdom of God. It is in the service of this Kingdom that the mission of Jesus and the apostles was carried out, and in its coming the truly catholic, complete community of all will become reality. In it there will no longer be any separation of the church from our life in the political realm.

5
Denominationalism and Christian Unity

I

The multiplicity of Christian denominations had its beginning in the division between Western Christianity and Eastern Orthodox Christianity. Perhaps, indeed, it can be traced back to the fifth century and the separation of the Monophysite and Nestorian churches. We might even say that the earlier division between the Orthodox and the Arian churches was denominational in character. But in Latin Christianity the multiplicity of denominations is a modern phenomenon, the result of the divisions that arose in the church in the sixteenth century, divisions that none of the "religious parties" of the time desired. In the sixteenth century the multiplicity of denominations was a multiplicity of mutually exclusive models of Christian unity. From the seventeenth to the nineteenth century this developed into a multiplicity of independent expressions of Christianity, which set themselves apart from one another as conservative versus modern, or as orthodox versus heretical. In the ecumenical movement of the twentieth century the multiplicity of denominations has once again been viewed in relation to the belief in the unity of the church, and it is easy to regard the various denominations as mere obstacles to Christian unity.

On the other hand, it must not be overlooked that the content of Christian beliefs and the forms of Christian life and church organization are today overwhelmingly intertwined

with the various denominational expressions of belief, practice, and organization. Thus there is a danger that a rejection of
denominational forms of faith and life would mean the loss of
that Christian content which has been preserved chiefly, or
even exclusively, in the specific forms it has assumed in
various denominations. Hardly ever does anyone contend
today that one of the denominations is the exclusive expression of the truth of the Christian faith and does not require
supplementation by the other Christian communities. In spite
of the contrasts in the ways the denominations express their
faith and life, they still preserve the substance of the traditional
Christian faith. Therefore, the denominations are more than
merely tenacious but outmoded remnants of a hopelessly
backward phase of Christian history, characterized by omi-
nous, even fatal divisions. At the very least, the denominations
can play a positive role in the future development of Christianity if they regard themselves as custodians of a heritage that
can be made a part of a new Christian unity. Viewed in this
way, the multiplicity of denominations has a positive function
today in the search for Christian unity. The challenge is to
allow the Christian substance preserved in contradictory denominational expressions to help shape a new awareness of
Christian community and share in the development of new
forms of Christian life. Even within the denominational
churches of today this will point beyond the differences of
earlier times. Critical principles must be established if we are
to evaluate the denominational traditions, and in order to
establish such principles we must reflect on what it really
means to confess the faith within the life of the church. Then in
that light we must examine the denominational expressions of
Christianity in our present-day churches.

II

A profession of faith in Christ stands at the center of all
confessing of the faith and all formation of creeds. It originates
in confession of Jesus Christ, of his message, and of his
person. Basically, it involves a personal community with Jesus
Christ, not a solemn assumption of responsibility to believe a

list of doctrines. In the Gospels this personal nature of confession is expressed in the words of Luke 12:8: "Every one who acknowledges *(homologēsē)* me before men, the Son of man also will acknowledge before the angels of God." Hans von Campenhausen has commented briefly on the "powerful subsequent history" of the saying: "In early Christianity, everywhere that we encounter a Christological confession, or a corresponding denial, we may assume that this saying of Jesus has had a direct or indirect effect."[5]

In what form did the earliest Christians confess their faith in Jesus? Was there any definite form? There has been uncertainty on the subject ever since Von Campenhausen presented significant arguments that cast doubt on the widespread assumption that the New Testament contains allusions to baptismal confessions, and even fragments of such confessions. He contends that it cannot be demonstrated that there were any baptismal confessions until well into the second century. Nonetheless, baptism as such constitutes an act of confessing one's faith in Jesus, and the "baptism of blood"—martyrdom—is such in the highest sense. It is doubtful, however, that the Christian employment for Jesus of such titles as Christ and Son of God can be considered as an act of confession, as Von Campenhausen and others assume. Not only does the verb "confess" seldom appear in connection with such titles but in addition the designation of Jesus by such exalted names was not necessarily appropriate to the public situation of a confession "before men." This is true also for the situation of the so-called "Great Confession" of Mark 8:29. That this text contains no specific indication that it is a confession weighs more heavily against calling it such than is usually acknowledged.

On the other hand, a frequently cited statement of Paul in Romans speaks directly of "confessing" and is often taken as a reference to a baptismal confession: "Because, if you confess with your lips that Jesus is Lord and believe in your heart that God raised him from the dead, you will be saved" (Rom. 10:9). Recently the cry "Jesus is Lord" has been designated as a cultic acclamation, to be distinguished from the form of a confession. Paul, however, specifically designates it a confession. If it is not possible to demonstrate the existence of a baptismal formula in the early church, and if even the Pauline formula is not to be understood as an allusion to a baptismal confession, then it is clear that the concept of a confession cannot be tied to this type of expression. The concept must be kept sufficiently open to take into account the specific and explicit Pauline usage. For Paul, confession of Jesus takes place when the worshiping community joins in acclaiming Jesus as Lord.

In contrast to Jesus' saying about confessing, Paul's statement provides the further information that when the worshiping community confesses faith in Jesus, this involves a closer designation of the object of faith than does the simple use of the name Jesus. The community is not simply confessing faith in Jesus, but in Jesus as Lord (Rom. 10:9). Similarly, the early Christian formula which Paul quotes in Philippians 2 ends with confession of Jesus as Lord and Christ (Phil. 2:11). This structure of confessing Jesus "as" Lord and Christ on the part of the community constitutes the starting point for the later development of baptismal and instructional confessions. In Romans, Paul adds that the confession of Jesus as Lord includes the belief in his resurrection by the power of God. Later this became one of the standard ways in which the content of the confession was made explicit.

Let us make completely clear the change that this set in motion. As long as Jesus with his proclamation was bodily present for everyone, it was not necessary to define more clearly the content of what it meant to confess him. To be sure, in the time before Easter his disciples may already have identified him as the expected Messiah (Mark 8:29), or as "the Son" of the Father, whom he proclaimed. These terms may already have expressed the meaning of Jesus for the disciples and may have served as the basis for confessing their faith in him. The decisive question of whether the one confessing his faith was really thereby confessing Jesus could at that time have been decided simply by whether Jesus accepted such a confession, and thus the varying interpretations of his person could remain unclarified. After Easter, however, the community had to use the interpretations attached to the name of Jesus in order to guarantee that the individual's confession was really directed to Jesus as the early church knew him. In this way the church stood in the place of Jesus, in that its acceptance of the individual's confession guaranteed that the person's confession was accepted by Jesus himself. In other words, the individual confessed faith in Jesus by affirming the confession of the community that Jesus was Lord, Christ, and Son of God. Thus the practice of specifying the meaning of Jesus by means of the interpretations connected with his person and work came to be the way in which the individual's confession was identified as truly directed to Jesus. Whether Jesus himself was truly the subject of the confession was now determined by whether the individual confessed Jesus in the same meaning as that by which the community expressed its unity with him. This explains how Paul could ascribe the nature of confession to participation in the acclamation of Jesus as Lord, as was customary in congregational worship. The confession of Jesus as the Son of God probably had a similar function, as seen in the First Epistle of John: "Whoever confesses that Jesus is the Son of God, God abides in him, and he in God" (I John 4:15). Here too the individual takes part in the activity of the community in which it calls Jesus the Son of God.

Confessing Jesus as the Son of God unites the individual not only with Jesus himself but also with God, according to First John. This is not some late statement of the early church; it is in agreement with the claim that Jesus himself made at the beginning of his ministry: that it was the relationship that people had to Christ that determined their relationship to God. By making this explicit, the statement in First John shows that confessing Jesus constitutes the starting point for the more complex baptismal confessions that later developed in the church. I John 2:23 points in the same direction: "He who confesses the Son has the Father also." In the Hellenistic world of polytheistic folk beliefs the confession of the Father as the one God assumed independent importance from the second century on, especially in the debates with the Gnostics, in which it was important to insist that this one God was the creator of the world. The differing developments of the confessions of faith in Christ resulted not only from the multiplicity of

titles connected with the name of Jesus but also from statements that God had raised Jesus from the dead (Rom. 10:9), or
that Jesus Christ had come in the flesh (I John 4:2).

Finally, just as confessing faith in Jesus involved the Father,
it also involved the Spirit, who had proceeded from Jesus and
who assured the believers of eternal life. Confessing Jesus as
Lord is the criterion of the true Spirit, for "no one can say
'Jesus is Lord' except by the Holy Spirit" (I Cor. 12:3). In the
period after Easter the act of confessing Jesus was performed
in the worship of the community that invoked the name of
Jesus; thus the confession of Jesus as the Son of God was
always at the same time the confession of the Spirit whom he
had sent and who was active in the church in which Jesus was
known as Lord and as Son of God. The trinitarian form of the
later Christian baptismal confessions (the starting point of
which can be seen in the Scriptures of the early church, Matt.
28:19) can be understood as the development of the confession
of Christ, as the development of the implications of a personal
confession of Jesus in terms of what he meant, specifically in
reference to his unity with God, which assured believers of
community with God. But it is also to be understood as the
development of the ecclesiastical nature of Christian confession. Henceforth the individual could confess Jesus only by
taking over the confession of the congregation to its Lord, and
also thereby confessing the work of the Spirit of Christ in this
congregation.

The process of expanding the content of the specific desig-
nations used in confessing faith in Jesus was clearly set in
motion by the debates with heretical beliefs which threatened
the clarity of the simple confession of Jesus as Lord, Christ,
and Son of God. This can be seen as early as First John and a
little later in the teachings of Ignatius of Antioch.[6] While Paul
could still rest content with the assumption that joining in the
acclamation of the congregation that "Jesus is Lord" implied
also the belief that God had raised him from the dead, First
John stressed the importance of the explicit confession that
Jesus had come in the flesh. In opposition to heretical teachings, this formula was a sign of the unity of Christians in their
confession of faith in Jesus Christ. A similar function was

served by the declarations of Ignatius. In participial clauses he summed up for the congregations to which he was writing the identity of the One whom they were confessing. The nuances of these formulations were determined by contemporary debates, and thus the human birth and the true suffering of Jesus received particular prominence. Ignatius was concerned that the church remain united in its confession of this Jesus Christ, and that no one fall victim to "vain, senseless teaching" (To the Magnesians 11). His comprehensive formulations contributed to the clarification of the essential content of the common faith of the church.

III

We have seen how the early Christian confessions combined two motifs: confessing faith in the person of Jesus and testifying to the meaning that formed the basis of such a confession. We have also seen how the acceptance of the meaning which united the community to Jesus guaranteed to the individual that his confession was truly directed to Jesus. This enables us to understand how important it was for the life of the church that there be unanimity in understanding the meaning ascribed to Jesus in the confessions. Whether one was in agreement concerning the meaning ascribed to Jesus, including his relationship to the Father and the Holy Spirit, was the measure of whether one was united to Jesus through the confession, so that through the community with Jesus the believers were united in community in Christ, in the unity of the church.

This enables us also to understand the function of the creedal statements of the ancient Catholic Church. At Nicaea in 325, at Constantinople in 381, and at Chalcedon in 451 the concern was to ensure that in the statements about Jesus Christ, about his relationship to the Father, and about the Holy Spirit, testimony was borne to the unity of believers in confessing Christ, and that thus the unity of the church was maintained.

Later theological development fulfilled the same function. To be sure, the dogmatic formulations of the medieval church did not always contain the entire confession of Christ. The independence of individual dogmatic topics from each other shows that doctrine had now become thematic. But there was always concern for the correctness of the doctrine, and ultimately for the meaning of Jesus for faith, even when doctrine was concerned with such specifics as grace, the sacraments, or anthropology. The same is true of the denominational confessions of the sixteenth and seventeenth centuries. Nevertheless, it is undeniable that in the course of these developments the increasingly differentiated problems of the doctrines about Jesus and of Christian doctrine in general took on an importance of their own. Thus it became difficult to recognize that such dogmatic definitions are ultimately concerned only with personal confession of faith in Jesus and with the identification of the conditions under which the community's confession of faith is to be acknowledged as such confession. This task now involves other interests in a "control of language" (Karl Rahner) for the church's theological teaching. Such control may be desirable for the sake of the unity of the church, even though it tends to conceal the possibility that the living plurality of interpretations of the Christian tradition might be endangered. In any case, it does not have the same value as the task of determining the conditions under which personal confession is made of faith in Jesus Christ.

The personal nature of that confession of faith must remain the central emphasis of all the statements of the church about confession. This does not mean that the elements of doctrine are excluded. Personal confession of faith in Jesus implies, as has been shown, an understanding of the meaning of Jesus and of the reality of God the Father and the Holy Spirit in unity with Jesus. In relation to these points of meaning, which themselves become the objects of instruction, the church and the individual reassure each other that the confession of Christian people is directed to one and the same Jesus Christ. But the instructional elements must retain their function as servants of the confession of faith. They are not the content of the church's confession in their own right. If the purpose of teaching were no longer distinguished from that of confessing, there would be a tendency to a doctrinal legalism, which would finally regard it as a failing if all the contents of Christian teaching were not fixed in creedal form. But such legalism must be recognized as a perversion of faith. No church confesses faith in a doctrine as such, but the Christian churches confess, by means of their teachings, their faith in the one Jesus Christ.

IV

The first consequence of this combination of content and the personal element in the act of confessing and also in the formulation of the church's confessions is that the various confessions of the churches must be judged in terms of their intentions. We must pose the question, To what extent can their dogmatic teachings claim to be conditions of a genuine unity of faith between the individual Christian and Jesus Christ? This question is urgent because the various churches with their controversies over one another's doctrinal confessions appeal to the same Jesus Christ, and intend to confess their faith in one and the same Jesus Christ.

The New Testament makes it possible to try to answer this question. The Gospels and the other documents of the apostolic age enable us to determine what the early church regarded as the condition of a confession of saving faith in Jesus, that is, faith that he is risen from the dead, that he is Lord and Christ, and that he came in the flesh. They also enable us to determine what Jesus himself taught, what the context of meaning was in which he made his appearance and lived his life, and, consequently, what a confession of faith in Jesus must involve in order truly to represent what we can know about Jesus, and not to allow an entirely different content to be confessed under his name.

It is widely accepted today that while the knowledge of the Scripture is not fully independent of the church's confessions and doctrines, it is still so to a large degree. The historical and critical study of biblical writings does not always lead to unanimous results, but it does follow its own methodological criteria and thus asserts its independence from the dogmatic exegesis of the churches in their teaching office and their creedal formulations. That the hermeneutical approach of each individual engaged in the scholarly exegesis of Scripture is determined by the person's presuppositions does not alter anything in this respect. The content itself corrects the presuppositions during the discussion of the various explanations of the text, and alternative explanations are measured by their ability to reveal the various aspects of the text and its context.

The possibility of judging the various forms of denominational teachings by their common subject matter through exegesis of the Scripture—that is, in terms of their intention to formulate conditions of the confession of faith in Jesus Christ—has more than a merely negative relevance for the evaluation of the church's creeds. In this case the formation of the church's doctrine would not be able to go beyond the statements of the Scripture. In reality, however, the content of the church's creeds cannot be limited to the statements of the early church, because the formation of the church's creeds involved the conditions necessary for a confession of faith in Christ in a later age, in the context of the language and problems of that age. It is in this context that we must evaluate the importance generally ascribed to the appearance of heresies as the occasion for the formation of creeds or dogmas. The specific relationship of each creed to a definite historical situation justifies one in going beyond the statements of the Bible, but it also limits the claims of such formulations to validity. A later phase of church history will in turn be determined by another set of problems, so that the specific elements in a confession of Christ will again be in need of reformulation.

But how is it possible to maintain the unity, the identity of the content of faith in view of the great difference among the confessions and creeds of the various epochs of the church's history? It is possible only if each succeeding age interprets all earlier confessional statements as expressions of the basic Christian intention to confess faith in Jesus Christ. It is necessary to let the personal intention of each confession of faith in Christ serve as the hermeneutical key to the understanding of its statements. This is the only way to perceive the actual unity of the confessional statements of the various ages of the church. We will then be able to evaluate the historical relativity of each doctrinal formulation without allowing our interpretation to remain caught in historical relativism.

As a result we will be able to deal in a basically similar manner with the differing creeds of the various denominations, which often contain statements diametrically opposed to each other. Such statements, even though when they were composed they represented mutually exclusive disagreements, now have become accessible to a productive interpretation, which reads those earlier contradictions in the light of their intention, namely, that both were attempts to formulate the conditions under which the confession of faith would correspond to the reality of Jesus Christ. Although the contrasting formulations of such conditions were then in conflict, they both referred to faith in the one and the same Jesus Christ. We can therefore begin by assuming that both parties to the conflict—for example, the Lutherans of the sixteenth century and the fathers of the Council of Trent, or the Lutherans and the Reformed theologians of the sixteenth and seventeenth centuries—were ultimately talking about the same Jesus Christ, even though the differences between their theological perspectives kept them from recognizing that fact. In the light of our present knowledge of Christ, we can describe how each side was then trying to deal with the reality of Jesus Christ, the reality which we perceive today in the perspective of our present experience on the basis of the New Testament texts.

Such an interpretation of the controversial doctrinal statements of the various denominations enables us to accept the content of these statements in a form that can be understood in the light of today's historical and exegetical knowledge. We can understand it as an expression of faith in Christ and as the identification of conditions for such faith, so that the confession of faith will correspond to the reality of Jesus Christ. If the intended meaning of the various doctrines and confessions can be shown to be the same, that is, concerned with the one reality of Jesus Christ, then the mutual excommunications of the past ages can be overcome. There are today efforts to reach a productive interpretation of the opposing doctrinal traditions without falsifying their positive intentions, as, for example, in the Leuenberg Agreement, even though the methodological presuppositions of such an undertaking have not yet been adequately set forth. In my opinion, this undertaking is important because we must read traditional dogmatic statements as confessional texts, that is, read them in terms of their personal intention to be confessions of faith in Christ. We should take them at their word as formulations of the conditions for a relevant and correct confession of faith, and we should follow the hermeneutical assumption that they were truly concerned with the correctness of our confession of faith in Christ. This assumption then becomes the key to investigating the normative content of these statements. A productive interpretation of this sort goes beyond the limited horizon of a purely historical hermeneutic that is directed toward only the meaning that was intended at that time. This can be compared with the juristic hermeneutic that explains a legal text in terms of the matter which it was intended to regulate and is not content merely to try to determine the subjective positions of the legislator. Such an interpretation would seek to determine whether and how the intentions of traditional confessional formulas lead us beyond the form of statements conditioned by their own time and bring us to confess faith in Christ.

V

A second insight can be derived from the conclusion that the doctrinal elements in the traditional confessional formulas and present-day confessions as well must be brought into relationship with the personal intention of confessing faith in Christ, so that they can continue to function toward realizing the completeness of our confession of faith in Christ. That is, the acceptance of a dogmatic formula does not mean the same thing as a personal confession of faith in Jesus Christ. The acceptance of such a formula, in which a church has expressed its understanding of the meaning of Jesus, cannot serve as more than a basis for the assumption that the one accepting the formula intends to confess faith in Jesus Christ. This basis is, however, by no means adequate in every case. The verdict on the authenticity of a personal confession is ultimately a spiritual and pastoral verdict. This is especially the case in admitting or excluding a person from the Lord's Supper. Excommunication is a spiritual decision, related to a person, and it is not appropriate to arrive at a verdict of excommunication in general terms, on the basis of conformity or lack of conformity with an approved confession of faith. Such an action does not consider that the acceptance or rejection of such a formulation can be the result of a variety of motives. In many cases the acceptance of the dogmas of the church is little more than the expression of a spirit of conformity that tells us little about the individual's spiritual involvement. On the other hand, there can be no doubt that frequently the creeds of certain churches were rejected or ignored by individual Christians and by entire communities, because they had, or were thought to have, nothing to do with the intention of confessing faith in Christ. This can be understood only in terms of the historical limitations of those doctrinal statements, unless we want to cling to the interpretation common in the age of the religious wars, that all truth was to be found on only one side. But, as has been pointed out, if each of us seeks the basis for unity in the developments of our own denominational tradition, we still cannot escape the recognition of the historical limitations and conditions to which the church's doctrinal statements are subject. The heart of the matter—that which was revealed in Jesus—transcends the limitations which each age imposes on the doctrinal statements it produces. And on the other hand, our faith and our personal confession of Christ are unconditioned and transcend the provisional nature of every form in which faith is confessed and every form in which the church's doctrines are formulated.

What conclusions can we draw on the basis of this discussion? The unity of the church is not primarily a unity of doctrine. It rests on a common confession of Jesus Christ. Differences and even contradictions in the way that Christians understand the faith do not necessarily negate the fact that we share a common confession of faith. Such contradictions could be regarded as contrasting expressions of what is basically the intention to hold the same faith, expressions that correct and supplement each other. To be sure, they could also be regarded as expressions of contradictions that invalidate our confession of Christ, that is, expressions that the other person is confessing something other than faith in Jesus Christ. Which of these is the case must finally be decided by a spiritual verdict on the situation in which such contradictions arise. In terms of a doctrinal confession, contradictions that we previously tolerated in our understanding of the faith can come to be seen as contradictions in our confession of Christ himself. On the other hand, disagreements that were once regarded as crucial to our confession of faith in Christ may, in the light of a later time, lose their force and validity.

According to the verdict of the authors of the Leuenberg Agreement, this is the case today with the issues that divided Protestants in the age of the Reformation. The differing, and in part opposing, doctrines of the Lutheran and Reformed churches of the sixteenth and early seventeenth centuries are today only traditional elements in the changed context of church life and theological discussion. Thus in a perspective that recognizes on both sides the intention to confess faith in Jesus Christ, we can say that in today's total picture the disagreements of that age have lost any significance great enough to divide churches. Such a verdict does not imply that we have found a solution to those once controversial questions, a solution that overcomes all the old differences and is accepted as valid by all sides. The consensus formulas of Leuenberg may well assume a higher degree of unanimity than actually exists in present-day theological discussion. But the decisive point is whether within the framework of the total situation today in discussions on the church and theology we can recognize, in contrast to the verdict of the sixteenth and seventeenth centuries, that in their formulations of doctrine both the Reformed and the Lutheran churches were concerned to confess their faith in Jesus Christ, and that in spite of the disagreements in their understanding of faith, no deviation from that intention can be detected. This verdict is capable of an intellectual justification, but it is essentially a spiritual verdict, which can take definitive form only through the efforts of the churches and their offices, and not through those of individual theologians, however much preparatory work the latter may be able to do. Such a spiritual verdict will first of all give legitimacy to a productive interpretation of past denominational divisions, so that both sides, despite their formerly exclusive claims, can produce their still one-sided but now mutually supplementary formulations of the confession of faith in the one Lord Jesus Christ.

6
The Reformation
and the Unity of the Church

The nineteenth-century celebrations of the Reformation looked back on it as a victory over the papal church of the Middle Ages and as the origin of modern Christianity. They celebrated the rediscovery of the gospel of the free grace of God and of the freedom of the individual conscience and faith that resulted from it. Today it is no longer possible to glorify the Reformation in so absolute a manner. We can no longer regard the Roman Catholic Church, as did nineteenth-century Protestants, as a fossil of the Middle Ages, as a form of Christianity left behind by history. The new ecumenical sensitivity of our century makes us more aware of the shadows that accompany the light of the Reformers' insights. We are aware of the unforeseen consequences of the Reformation—the bloody wars of religion of the sixteenth and seventeenth centuries, and the division of Western Christianity, which became final after the indecisive conclusion of those bitter struggles. It was as a consequence of the division of the church that there developed a world free from all religious ties, a world in which the theory of the state, in union with changing political ideologies, established its independence, and economic forces were allowed to follow their own laws. The wars of mutual annihilation waged by the "religious parties" of the Reformation age made it inevitable that the bases of human life in community would be reconstituted in a manner that made them independent of the quarrels of various denominations. Today, when the internal weakness of this world of modern secular culture is evident, we must recognize in it the delayed results of the division of the church. The separation of the modern world from those questions which have been relegated to the private sphere of religion reveals that world as a colossus with feet of clay, because the ordering of human life in community is increasingly divorced from any basis in a universally binding sense of duty.

It is no longer possible to think of the Reformation without also thinking of the fragmentation of the Western church and its consequences, including the problems of our contemporary secular culture. These are the undesired consequences of the Reformation but it is because of these consequences that the Reformation has exerted such incomparable influence on world history. Nothing was farther from the desires of the Reformers than the separation of the various Protestant churches from the one catholic church. The establishment of a separate Protestant Christianity was a makeshift solution, because the original goal of the Reformation was the reform of the entire church. By that standard, the rise of specific Evangelical and Reformed churches marked not the success of the Reformation but its failure. The Protestant churches of our day and their official leaders should keep this fact constantly in mind. This realization, that the existence of separate Protestant churches alongside the Roman Catholic Church testifies to the failure of the Reformation, is well suited to guarding against that complacency which was characteristic of so much earlier Protestant thought about the Reformation.

Luther expressed his desire to maintain the unity of the church especially in the period before 1520. In 1519, two years after the Ninety-five Theses, he held it as an "inexcusable reproach" against the Hussites that they had created a schism by resisting the authority of the pope on insufficient grounds (*WA* 2, 186). As late as 1520, Luther was willing to kiss the pope's feet, if only he would accept the doctrine of justification, as Luther had set it forth in his tractate *The Freedom of a Christian Man*. He expressed a similar willingness in 1531 (*WA* 40/1, 181). Luther, who felt that he had been called to interpret the Scripture, believed that in this doctrine he had discovered the heart of the gospel. As an exegete he believed that he was bound in conscience to it, so after the doctrine had been definitively rejected by the pope, he came more and more to regard the pope as the enemy of the gospel itself, and as the Antichrist, whose mark it is, according to II Thess. 2:4, that he "opposes and exalts himself against every so-called god or object of worship, so that he takes his seat in the temple of God, proclaiming himself to be God." If, and insofar as, the pope opposes the gospel, and especially the article of justification through Christ, without merit, by faith alone, then these marks of the Antichrist fit him. Yet even here the Reformation did not basically reject a supreme office in the church. In his well-known comment on the Schmalkald Articles of 1537, Melanchthon declared that if the pope would "accept the gospel . . . for the sake of peace and unity, . . . then he would allow and acknowledge his superiority over the bishops, which he exercises by human law (jure humano)." Melanchthon's *Apology for the Augsburg Confession* (1530) expressed the readiness of Protestants to submit to the jurisdiction of the bishops, on the condition that they would accept the doctrine of justification. In reference to subjection under the jurisdiction of the bishops there was the further condition that they accept those Protestant preachers who had been ordained in the meantime and whose ordination was termed an emergency measure in order to provide oversight for the congregations that had arisen.

The widespread readiness of Protestants, after decades of bitter conflicts, to submit to the episcopal order of the medieval church and to accept the primacy of the pope, if only he would not oppose the gospel, is an impressive documentation of the desire of the Reformers to preserve or restore the unity of the church. This picture is supplemented by the deep concern of the Reformers to stress their agreement with the dogmas of the early church, as expressed in the solemn repetition of the ancient creeds in the Augsburg Confession regarded as the only disagreement that Protestants had with the medieval church. In the light of these concerns to preserve the unity of the church, it is impossible to deny that the Reformation was concerned to bring about the renewal of all Christendom on the basis of the gospel, and not to create separated Protestant churches. But then it is impossible to avoid the conclusion, which I have advanced above, that the establishment of Protestant churches in the sixteenth century and the resulting divisions in the Western church mark, not the success of the Reformation, but its failure. At the very least, the Reformation remained unfinished in the sixteenth century, and it will remain unfinished until the unity of a truly catholic church, renewed by the gospel of Jesus Christ, is finally restored.

In the centuries since the Reformation, Protestants have been only dimly aware of this fact. Why has this been so? Above all, undue emphasis has been placed on the Reformation formula of "pure doctrine" *(pura doctrina)* as the basis of the true church and its unity. The classic Protestantism of the late sixteenth through the eighteenth century underestimated the difficulty of arriving at an unequivocal understanding of the doctrinal contents of the scriptural documents. It did not see the differing perspective of the biblical books, conditioned by their varying situations, nor did it see that later exegesis was dependent on the perspective of its own time and on that of the individual exegete. This also holds true for the controversial positions of the age of the Reformation itself. As a result, classic Protestantism could regard its own understanding of Scripture as the sole repository of the pure doctrine of the gospel, and regard the church founded on that consensus as the only true church. Thus the Protestant churches lost sight of the task of realizing a greater unity with all churches that confessed faith in Christ. Instead, they themselves split and split again. That this classic Protestant concept of an exclusive understanding of the true doctrine was untenable was made clear by modern historical-critical study of Scripture. But out of these critical insights (not to mention the stimulus of Schleiermacher and others) there developed, not a different understanding of the church, but a Protestant individualism which regarded the institutional church as completely outmoded and looked forward to a time when the church would be absorbed into a culture molded by Christian influences and into a moral political state. In this setting it is understandable that the unity of the Christian church was not regarded as a pressing problem. Nor was the situation different in the realm of a romanticized denominationalism that was concerned only with the renewal of one's own church tradition.

The ecumenical movement of our century has brought about a new awareness that the unity of the churches must be a vital concern of all Christians. This movement has various roots, above all the consciousness that Christians bear a common responsibility for the great social problems confronting humanity in our century, and the awareness of how intolerable Christian divisions are, especially in the mission field. Because the denominational traditions no longer had so strong a conviction of their exclusive validity, there was room for a new consciousness that all Christians belong together through their unity with their one Lord, who is not only the common source of all Christian churches but also—in spite of all divisions— their common future. And finally, in contrast to cultural Protestantism, there developed, especially in the realm of Reformation Christianity, a growing consciousness of the significance of the church for the Christian life of the individual. The political developments of the twentieth century have made it clear that the Christian life does not find fulfillment in an already existing culture formed under Christian influence, and that the church cannot as a consequence be absorbed more and more into the moral ordinances of the state. And thus Protestants must once again see the church as the form in which the Christian revelation is expressed in the life of this world and as the place where the faith of the individual Christian must find its expression. As a result, the question of the unity of the Christian church is posed with new urgency— the question of a truly catholic church, in which the unity of all Christians in their faith in Christ can find adequate expression.

A future church that unites all Christians cannot simply be identical with any one of today's denominational churches, separated as they are from one another by the anathemas of earlier centuries. Yet even so, that greater catholicity of the church of Christ can become visible in today's separated churches, just as the one catholic church manifests itself in the local church that is gathered for worship. This occurs in every place where the unity of all Christians in Jesus Christ is affirmed and celebrated in the faith of individual Christians and in life of the worshiping church. Is it not necessary to say that the church "subsists" everywhere in our still divided churches, as the Second Vatican Council said of the Roman Catholic Church? But if the one church of Christ is made evident in today's still separated churches, are we not compelled to give this unity clearer expression in the relation of the churches to one another? The one church of Christ can become manifest in the divided churches only to the extent to which they can acknowledge in theory and practice that the other churches and traditions also belong to Christ. In this area, each of the denominational traditions can make a special contribution toward the greater catholicity of a future form of the church that will unite all Christians. Each also has a contribution to make to a greater breadth of catholicity within each of our present separated churches.

What, then, is the specific contribution of the Reformation to this new catholicity or universality of the Christian faith which before our eyes is now coming into being among the separated churches? What is the contribution that the Reformation churches can make to the unity of all Christians? We have seen that such a question is so close to the intentions of the Reformers that we are really posing the question of the completion of the Reformation itself.

Again and again Luther brought the concerns of the Reformation together under the common denominator of a single theme. As late as 1537 he said of the article concerning justification "through Christ . . . without merit . . . by faith" that on it "rests everything which we teach in opposition to the pope, the devil, and the world." It is clear that this Lutheran doctrine of justification no longer divides the churches from one another in theological discussion. This is the result of the lifework of Joseph Lortz, as well as of a large number of studies, such as those of Hans Küng on Karl Barth and those of Otto H. Pesch on Luther's doctrine of justification. The view is extensively held today in Catholic studies of Luther that while Luther developed his thoughts in a mode unfamiliar to scholastic theology, still in their substance they express a fundamental Christian truth. They were misunderstood then because they were viewed from a traditional perspective. It is to be wished that this result of scholarly research might be tested, and, if possible, confirmed by the teaching office of the Catholic Church. According to many of Luther's statements, the doctrine of justification is the only one which he felt he had to maintain even against the opposition of the pope, doing so for the sake of his conscience, bound as it was by the Scripture. If the substance of this doctrine is accepted as Catholic, then the one reason which from the first was considered decisive for the separation of the Reformation churches from the Roman Catholic Church is eliminated. Official confirmation that this doctrine of Luther's is in accord with Catholic orthodoxy would thus have far-reaching consequences for the relationship of the Reformation churches to Rome.

Since the Catholic nature of the central doctrine of the Reformation that justification is by faith alone is widely accepted today, the question must be raised whether the division of the Western church with all its torments of conscience, all its bloodshed, its zeal for the faith on both sides, and its grievous consequences must be seen today as having resulted from a simple misunderstanding. This question cannot be answered with either a positive yes or a clear no. Beyond any doubt, misunderstandings played a major role—for instance, the misunderstanding which held that works of love were meaningless for anyone who confessed that justification was through faith alone. Luther's passionate nature did not make it easy to clear up such misunderstandings, but the real problem lies deeper. The hierarchical structure of authority in the medieval church was so constituted that division could result from open criticism of abuses which today are deplored by Catholics and from misunderstandings arising from unconventional theological formulations. The problems are (1) that condemnation could be made without a relevant testing of the condemned statements in their proper context, (2) that the possibility of a plurality of theological opinion was so limited, (3) that a new way of formulating one's understanding of the faith on the basis of scriptural exegesis could immediately be rejected as damnable, and (4) that, as in the Leipzig Disputation, the discussion could come to center on the question of the formal authority of pope and council, instead of continuing to deal with the question of the content of the gospel, the basis of Luther's arguments. To this extent the hierarchical, authoritarian structure of the medieval church was the real reason that a position based on one's own understanding of the gospel and the power of the truth over one's conscience, as in Luther's case, could ultimately lead to division of the church.

On the other hand, the doctrine of justification by faith in opposition to this hierarchical, authoritarian structure implied a direct relationship of the believer with God and a freedom based on trust in God that could stand against any human authority, whether ecclesiastical or political. This freedom constitutes the heart of the doctrine of justification, and the doctrine of justification is the theological formulation and basis of this freedom. Luther himself set this forth in 1520 in his pamphlet *The Freedom of a Christian Man*. But a direct relationship with God on the basis of faith, which assures the believer of such incomparable freedom, by no means excludes human mediation and the grateful acknowledgment of such mediation, nor does it involve unmediated, direct access to God. For Luther the public proclamation of the gospel and the church office charged with such proclamation were the indispensable means by which the individual comes to faith, and thus also the means of his direct access to God in full awareness of his Christian freedom. This explains the respect which Luther was so ready to accord the officers of the church without reference to their personal worthiness, as long as they did not oppose the gospel itself. A church office did not exist for its own sake. Its purpose was to serve the gospel and thus the faith of those entrusted to its care, in order to help them come to their own direct relationship with God, and not leave them in a state of immaturity. Thus human mediation and a direct relationship to God belong together, as do Christian freedom and the acknowledgment of the offices of the church and of the mutual intercession of believers for one another. Indeed, they belong very closely together.

This concept of Christian freedom is the most important heritage of the Reformation. The Protestant churches of today

must preserve it and bring it as their special contribution to a
new consciousness that includes all Christians. Perhaps one
day it will find its expression in a comprehensive catholicity, in
a form of the church that will unite all Christians and provide
room for their differing traditions. It is only Christian freedom
and what is inseparably connected with it in the heritage of the
Reformation that is worth preserving and transmitting to the
whole Christian world. Many features of the Reformation and
its theology were merely products of the age in which they
arose. I include there the one-sided concentration on confession and penitence, which tied the Reformation to the church
of the late Middle Ages and its theology, and which appear
foreign to modern thought. I further include a matter closely
connected with such confession, the specific form of the
distinction between law and gospel and their relationship to
each other as it was developed in Lutheran theology. This does
not correspond to the distinction between salvation in the age
of gospel and that in the age of law, as set forth in the
statements of Paul. Among the outmoded elements of the
Reformation I also include Luther's political theology, the
doctrine of the two realms, even though it contains, as do the
points mentioned above, elements of truth of abiding value.
These outmoded elements also include much of Luther's
polemic against the papacy and against the Mass. Even though
the polemic was justified in both cases, according to our
modern way of thinking it did not deal with the central issues,
either those of the Catholic Mass or those of the necessity of a
supreme and universal office in the church. Finally, Luther's
understanding of Scripture and the related concept of the
relationship of faith to the word of God are also outmoded.
Since the rise of the historical-critical method of biblical study,
it is no longer possible for us to find the word of God itself in
the words of Scripture in as direct a manner as Luther could.
This overvaluing of the direct nature of divine authority in the
Scriptures in Luther's thought is related to a certain degree
(we will return to this point later) to his underestimating of the
role of human mediation in divine revelation. Basically, Luther
saw the necessity of such human mediation in the proclamation of the gospel. He was able to emphasize, not only in the

history of the church but also in the Scripture itself, the purely human element of such mediation. Yet the full implications of the fact that we have God's revelation only by means of human mediation were not yet seen, and indeed in his age it was not possible to see them fully. Thus it is all the more important that the central Reformation discovery of Christian liberty based on the immediacy of faith in God loses nothing of its force and its decisive significance through the recognition of human mediation, as long as the result and the meaning of all such human mediation is to bring the individual into a direct relationship to God through faith, a relationship that corresponds to God's coming to men and women in Jesus Christ.

For me the special contribution which the churches of the Reformation can make to the whole of Christianity is to preserve the concept of Christian freedom, this precious heritage of the Reformation, to consider what is necessary for its existence, and to develop its consequences. This is true in reference to the relationship of Christian faith to the life of society, in reference to a legitimate pluralism in our understanding of the faith, and the resulting freedom for the offices of the church and the constitution of church life in general. The ecumenical tasks that result from this central theme of the Reformation are particularly urgent today.

In the modern period, the triumph of the idea of Christian freedom in the Reformation became the historical starting point for the development of the modern concept of freedom as a whole. It served as the catalyst for the development of civil liberties in the English revolution of the seventeenth century and in the early constitutional documents in America. In the further development of the modern consciousness of freedom, however, the Christian bases of this freedom as they found lively expression in the Reformation concept of "Christian freedom" have been largely neglected. The reasons for this need not be gone into here, but they are mainly the consequences of the divisions of the churches. Neglect of the bases of the Christian concept of freedom is an empty form of arbitrary individualism. In the long run, this loss of content will discredit the concept of freedom itself. Many Christians take delight in regarding the pluralistic freedom of today as the outgrowth of the Reformation concept of Christian freedom. It must be admitted that without the process of church division and secularization, freedom based on the Christian faith could not have been adapted to the realities of the world. That process also involved liberating the concept of freedom from its religious roots. But because it has been the fate of freedom to become something merely formal, devoid of content, there is a danger that it will sink into the banality of individual arbitrariness and then finally become the provocation for a new totalitarian attempt to give meaning to the life of society.

In this situation the task of preserving the Christian bases of modern freedom requires us to consider anew the Christian church as the place where Christian freedom has its origin. Because of the separation between religion and the state, political life offers little chance for bringing about a realization of the universal validity of the basis and understanding of the concept of freedom. Therefore the task of the Reformation churches in the present day demands more than just the preservation of their heritage in intellectual terms; it must also bring about the renewal of a catholicity that embraces all of Christianity and is expressed in the church's worship and in its organizational structures. The Christian freedom that lives through the confidence that God is accessible to all mankind in Christ needs the church as its own proper realm of expression. But it is only in community with all Christians and with the apostolic origins of the church that it can find its ecclesiastical home. Faith cannot exist without love. The individual Christian cannot be sure of unity with Jesus Christ without unity with all Christians and without an openness to all mankind, an openness that is possible for the individual only as a member of the community of Christ. Just as the Protestant churches must bring the concept of Christian freedom as their particular contribution to the whole Christian church, so too they must integrate the distinctive contributions of other traditions and churches into their own life. Only so can the Reformation be brought to completion through overcoming our inherited divisions in a new, ecumenical, and therefore truly catholic church that includes all Christians.

In the ecumenical conversations of recent decades, but

especially since the Second Vatican Council, the representatives of the churches of the Reformation have participated in such an adaptation of pan-Christian elements for their own understanding of the church. This is true, above all, for the rediscovery of the central significance which the Eucharist has for the worship of all Christian churches, except for that of some Protestant communions. The ecumenical encounters of our time show that this is an area where the Reformation churches have been impoverished. This is not something which the great Reformers desired, but it developed through opposition to the Roman Mass and through concentration on the proclamation of the word in Protestant churches. This impoverishment of our worship must be overcome through a renewal of our awareness of the central significance of the Eucharist for the life of the church. It is not by chance that the ecumenical conversations between theologians of the Reformation churches and theologians of the Catholic and Orthodox churches have concentrated on the theme of the Lord's Supper and on the basis for unity in observing it. In the Lord's Supper the present divisions in the church and the senselessness of these divisions are more apparent than anywhere else, and in all this the broken and distorted nature of the church that results from these divisions finds expression. In recent years the ecumenical dialogue in several lands has turned from discussion of the Lord's Supper to the parallel question of church offices. This too has not come about by chance. After extensive clarification of the dogmatic problems connected with the Lord's Supper, the real center of the difficulties that still prevent a full mutual sharing in the Lord's Supper became evident. It is the connection between the celebration of the Eucharist in worship and the community of the church as expressed in the official structures of the various churches, especially in the authority of specific office-bearers to administer the Eucharist. Thus conversations have concentrated on church offices in general, and more recently have been concerned especially with the office of bishop and the question of a supreme office in the church with responsibility for all of Christianity.

Luther and the Lutheran theologians of the Reformation

period dealt only in limited fashion with such questions, even though these questions involved the church's transmission and application of the doctrine of justification and the Christian freedom of the individual. Luther did deal with the significance of the "outer word" *(verbum externum)* and thus with the office of the public proclamation of the gospel, just as he dealt elsewhere with the necessity of fellowship among believers as the result of the fellowship each of them had with Christ. These were ideas that he developed in his sermons of 1519 in close connection with the sacrament of the altar. But neither Luther nor Melanchthon found a central place in their ecclesiology for the relationship of the Eucharist to the office of bishop and to the unity of the church. Perhaps the primary reason for this was the direct nature of divine authority in the biblical word and in its proclamation, as well as the understanding of how the word as addressed to the individual could bring repentance. A related factor was the individualistic nature of the Reformation observance of the Lord's Supper, according to which the Lord's Supper was primarily the concrete assurance of Christ's forgiveness to the individual. This was probably the starting point for the later loss of significance of the Lord's Supper in Protestant worship. And just as the ecclesiological relevance of the Lord's Supper—its connection with the unity of the congregation and with Christians in general—was largely neglected, so too the church lost sight of the responsibility of the bishop for the unity of his community in the total context of the life of the whole church.

On the basis of the Reformation theology of the word, the offices of the church were one-sidedly identified with the public proclamation of the gospel—the preaching office. The other tasks of the office-bearer—to care for the unity of the community entrusted to him, to coordinate different developments, to relieve tensions, and in his person, in what he did and what he said, to give expression to the unity of his community—were not denied, but they were not explicitly regarded as essential tasks of the officers of the church. The Reformers regarded all pastors as bishops, in imitation of the early church as it was described by the church father Jerome. According to him, there was in the early church, especially in

Alexandria, no essential difference between priests and bishops. By this use of terminology they wished to preseve the episcopal structure of the offices of the church. In addition, the Reformers were ready, as I have pointed out, to recognize the authority of superior church officers, especially bishops, who in the medieval church had become regional administrators. The Reformers recognized that bishops had the authority to ordain, although priests had had to carry out emergency ordinations in order to provide pastors for congregations that had newly arisen. Not only did the Reformers not reject the regional office of the medieval bishops, but they did not in principle reject the universal office, the superiority of the pope over the bishops.

The main point of contention in those days was whether this superiority was based on divine law or human law. This is no longer of importance for our present discussion, if we recognize that the very limited use of the concept "divine law" in the Reformation is connected with the view that the Scripture is the sole source of divine law. On the other hand, the necessity of the office of bishop and the necessity of a high regard for the office of unity among Christians can be based on the nature of the church itself as the community of Christians with one another, founded on their community with Christ. The Reformation declarations, however, do not have their own theology of the office of bishop or of pastor in relationship to the question of church unity, either in regard to the inner structure of the local congregation and its worship or in regard to the relationship of the individual congregation with all other congregations and with the whole development of the church from the time of the apostles. These points of view are implicit in the Reformation declarations concerning the church and church offices, but they were not developed as explicit themes. The Augsburg Confession of 1530 regarded questions of the structure of church offices as matters relating to the external structure of the church, which were not determined by the nature of the church. Thus in Article 7 it says that it is sufficient (*satis est*) to the unity of the church that there be agreement concerning the pure teaching of the gospel and the proper observance of the sacraments. The Lutheran bishop

Hans Heinrich Harms has commented succinctly, " *'Satis est'* *non satis est.*" In reality, the organization of the church is not a secondary, external matter, in that it involves making visible the unity which believers have with one another through their unity with Christ. In this light there has developed on the Protestant side of the ecumenical dialogue a new understanding of the theology of the office of bishop and of the Eucharist as the center of the worshiping community. But Protestant congregations and denominations must bring the Catholic tradition of Christianity to fuller realization and exemplify it more fully, in the same way that on the Catholic side today the church at all levels must strive to see that its own institutions are permeated by the idea of Christian freedom.

Such a process of convergence in the central features of church life brings the realization of the community of faith founded on Christ. In this way we will be most likely to come nearer to the moment when the mutual recognition of our churches as member churches of the one church of Christ will be possible. Only then will the church be able to be in the fullest sense the "sign and implement of the unity of mankind," as the Second Vatican Council said and the World Council of Churches Assembly in Uppsala in 1968 reaffirmed in almost identical words. "Sign and instrument of the unity of mankind"—*sacramentum unitatis*—this the church cannot be in its divided state. It can be this only if Christians, despite all the differences of their traditions, are ready to join in recognizing that they are one in Christ, and so discover one another in unity in him. In this way they would solve the great human problem of the unity of freedom and community for the shared life of Christians, and thereby they could present the Christian community as an example of the way all mankind should live together.

7
An Ecumenical Understanding
of the Church's Offices

*A lecture on the significance of the Memoran-
dum of the University Ecumenical Institutes,
Spring 1973, delivered at the Institute for European History in Mainz, January 16, 1974*

In recent years ecumenical discussions have concentrated to
a remarkable degree on the questions of the understanding of
church offices and of the possibility of mutual recognition of
church offices, or even on a full, "organic" unity of the
church. The tendency to concentrate on these questions is less
noticeable at the level of the World Council of Churches. It is
true that even there since the conference in New Delhi in 1961
and especially since that in Montreal in 1963, discussion of the
question of church offices has been revived in the Commission
on Faith and Order. Still, other questions occupy the foreground, and the Commission's work on this question has
produced only preliminary results. By contrast, since 1970 the
findings of a series of bilateral conversations between
churches of the Reformation and the Roman Catholic Church
over the question of church offices have been published, and
they converge in a remarkable manner toward the possibility
of mutual recognition of church offices. In addition to such
discussions in the United States and in France, attention
should be called to the so-called Malta Report of the Evangelical Lutheran and Roman Catholic study commission of 1971.
These concerns were also shared by the Memorandum of the
German University Ecumenical Institutes.

At present the most important starting point for this concentration on the problem of church offices is to be found in the
growing interest in the churches in the question of intercommunion. The major factor preventing it today is the lack of

mutual recognition of the validity of church offices. A study by the Faith and Order Commission of the World Council of Churches says, "Everyone who has experienced this painful separation at the celebration of the Eucharist will naturally be led to take this problem seriously."[7] In addition to this existential motivation for ecumenical concern with the theology of church offices there is a whole list of additional factors, two of which deserve particular attention. The first is the new insight that grew out of the New Delhi conference of 1961 that no form of church unity is possible without prior progress in the question of the mutual recognition of church offices. The second is to be found in the statements of the Second Vatican Council concerning the churches that are separated from Rome, statements that seem to include a certain degree of positive evaluation of the offices in these communities, and whose possible ecumenical influence has been the subject of detailed discussion.

The specific starting point of the joint work of the German University Ecumenical Institutes (the first product of which was the Memorandum on Church Offices) was the ongoing joint work of the two Munich institutes, especially a report published in 1970 on the results of a joint seminar on the theme "The Offices of the Church."[8] Reflections on these results by members of the German University Ecumenical Institutes soon led to the conclusion that it was possible to reach extensive agreement among the various institutes on the basic features of an interpretation of church offices, and in the light of the central significance of this problem for ecumenical discussion the institutes were of the opinion that they should bring their agreement to the attention of a wider audience of theologians and church leaders. This seemed particularly urgent, since in efforts toward intercommunion reference was made again and again, particularly by those representing the offices of the church, to the continuing denominational disagreement over church offices as a fact generally recognized by theologians. The increasing agreement in the understanding of church offices that had been attained in the conversations of the various international study commissions was hardly known at all in Germany. These study commissions had begun their work independently of one another, but their results had increasingly converged, as had the conclusions reached by the German institutes. This was quite different from the general assumption that a theology of church offices involves a hard core of intractable disagreements, especially between the Roman Catholic Church and the Protestant churches, not realizing that here, as in other traditional controversies, such as the doctrine of justification, a mutual theological understanding was attainable. The ecumenical institutes felt that they were obligated to develop and make public their consensus on church offices. One reason for this was that they felt they shared the responsibility for preventing one-sided assumptions about "insuperable theological obstacles" from slowing down further progress toward ecumenical understanding among the churches.

In terms of this starting point it is possible to understand a distinctive feature of the Memorandum on Church Offices which distinguishes it from the reports of the various ecumenical study commissions. The Memorandum attempts to express the positive consensus of the institutes involved through mutually acceptable theses on the understanding of church offices. The Memorandum therefore does not contain a description of the various denominational conceptions of office, as are found in the reports of the ecumenical study commissions. Some have complained of the lack of such a description,[9] but such criticism misunderstands the purpose of the Memorandum. Its purpose was to present an example of how it was possible for Protestants and Catholics to join together in presenting a theology of church offices. In working toward such a goal the description of the existing denominational differences cannot be a major objective. These differences were spoken of only insofar as they were overcome through mutual formulations, but in loyalty to the theological positions of both denominational traditions it was important to understand them.

From this it should be clear—indeed, it should already have been obvious—that the consensus formulated in the theses of the Memorandum merely expressed the consensus of the institutes involved. It neither can nor should substitute for or prejudge actions and decisions of the responsible church authorities. It can, however, serve as preparation for such actions and decisions by documenting the possibility of an understanding of church offices developed by Protestant and Catholic theologians.

Moreover, the Memorandum does not present the full content of a doctrine of church offices. That would involve a more detailed treatment of the various forms of offices that have developed in the history of the church, especially the office of bishop. Walter Kasper, in his discussion of the Memorandum, rightly pointed out this lack.[10] The continuing significance of the office of bishop is not an explicit theme of the Memorandum, although this question is certainly of great ecumenical significance. This is also true of the problem of papal primacy. Karl Rahner in particular felt that it was a major flaw that this problem was not discussed.[11] The Memorandum was limited to consideration of the question of the distinctive nature of ordination, without going into the three-fold structure of the office, or considering the theme of the office of bishop or that of the primacy of the pope. This does not mean that the specific approach of the Memorandum to the question of ordination does not have implications of consider-able significance for the question of the office of bishop and the question of a supreme office in the universal church. More will be said later on these questions.

In reference to the Memorandum's statements on the Holy Spirit it should also be stressed that it does not contain a complete doctrine of church offices. The question is expressly placed in the context of the Pauline doctrine of charismatic gifts. It stresses that through the gift of the Spirit each member of the church "is called to a particular service" (Thesis 9), that the call to these differing services is given through "the power of the one Spirit of Jesus Christ" (Thesis 14), and that according to the New Testament such service "is to be understood as the gift of the Spirit of God for the service of the community, that is, as a charismatic gift" (Thesis 8). As a consequence, the special service of leadership of the congrega-tion should be performed in "the Spirit of Jesus Christ" (Thesis 12). In view of these statements, it is astonishing that

Karl Lehmann, in his comments on Thesis 15, even though there too the concept of charisma is taken up, objects that the "invocation of the Spirit and the bestowal of the gift of the Spirit for the service of the church" "is explicitly mentioned neither here nor elsewhere in the Theses."[12] It is true that the invoking of the Spirit, the epiclesis, is not explicitly discussed in connection with ordination, although in the Lutheran ordination rite it also has a place. This theme could be omitted in the Memorandum because Catholic theology and Reformation theology do not disagree on this point, aside from the questions involving the sacramental nature of ordination, which are treated separately. Moreover, the traditional differences between the Catholic and the Reformation understanding of church offices cannot be overcome on the basis of the doctrine of the Holy Spirit. It is not only ordination that is a gift of the Spirit but also the other forms of service in the church. The question of the distinctive nature of ordination will not find its answer here.

It is this problem which is central in the Memorandum. This is certainly not amiss, in the light of the conclusion of the Second Vatican Council that the office of priest differs from the universal priesthood of all believers not only in degree but also in its very essence (*Lumen Gentium* II. 10). This contention presents considerable difficulties for Protestant thought, because it seems to elevate the office-bearer above the fellowship of believers instead of expressing the distinctive nature of his service within this community and in relationship to it. For this reason the Arnoldshain Conference, in its position paper on the Memorandum of the Ecumenical Institutes, stresses that the special service of the ordained offices does not differ "in its essence" from the authority which is given to the church as a whole" (§4). And in his essay on "The Lutheran Understanding of Church offices," the Oldenburg bishop, Hans Heinrich Harms, chairman of the Arnoldshain Conference, wrote that the universal priesthood of all believers and the offices of the church are "the same in essence."[13]

Do we have here a significant disagreement with the formula of the Second Vatican Council, one that goes beyond a mere disagreement over terminology? In any case, ecumenical discussion must seek to elucidate more clearly than has been done thus far the distinctive nature of ordained offices in the Lutheran churches. That this involves a difference from other functions that is not merely one of degree but is a qualitative and essential distinction should not cause offense to Protestants, if such a difference in essence is a part of the larger context of the life of believers in community. The relationship between the priesthood of all believers and specific offices in the church is thus clearly of especial significance for ecumenical understanding between Catholics and Protestants in their understanding of church offices. It is dealt with explicitly in Thesis 15 of the Memorandum and in the related preliminary study (pp. 191, 199ff.). This problem is also present in the other theses of the Memorandum, although expressed in other terms, that is, in those of the Pauline doctrine of charismatic gifts. This terminology has the advantage that it does present the special offices of the church in isolated contrast to the participation of all believers in the priesthood of Christ, but presents it alongside other, concrete functions, which are also specific gifts of the Spirit as are the ordained offices. What, then, constitutes the distinctive nature of ordination?

In its answer to this question the Memorandum unites a "Catholic" component with a "Protestant" one. It describes the ordained office as the service office of leadership, which consists in the "public expression of the common concern" of all Christians (Thesis 12), that is, their "participation in the mission of Christ" (Thesis 15). The description of the ordained office as one of leadership for the congregation has an unfamiliar sound for Protestants. The Arnoldshain Conference took what is otherwise a very positive position to the Memorandum of the Ecumenical Institutes, but it protested that the Memorandum speaks "of the task of leading the congregation through one or more ordained officers as something beyond dispute" (§3). On the Protestant side the task of proclamation is generally taken as the only constitutive task of the church's officers. The report of the Arnoldshain Conference continued, "The question of the relationship between the authority of proclamation and that of leadership exercised in common with nontheologians is in need of further clarification."

It is significant that the Memorandum characterizes church offices not in terms of the task of proclamation but as responsible for leading the congregation, and then within this characterization emphasized "the proclamation of the word, together with the administration of the sacraments, and the active involvement in the life of church and society" as being "basic" (Thesis 12). This constitutes a broadening of the usual Protestant understanding of church offices. In Protestant thought the task of the officer to proclaim the gospel is often conceived in such narrow terms that the task of leading the congregation appears to be something different, a mere supplement. As a result, the responsibility of leading the congregation can be regarded as theologically neutral and left to merely pragmatic considerations. It seems, however, that the statements of the Augsburg Confession of 1530 concerning church offices implicitly regard it as obvious that the function of leading the congregation is involved in the responsibility of proclamation. According to the Augsburg Confession (Art. 28), the latter included not only the responsibility for pronouncing the forgiveness of sins, and thus the power of the keys, but also the responsibility for judging doctrines and administering church discipline. These are functions that clearly have the aim of preserving or restoring the oneness of the community in the teachings of the gospel. But they do not belong, in the strict sense of the word, to the task of proclamation. If we were to give a comprehensive characterization of these functions, it would seem appropriate to say that the office-bearer has responsibility for the unity of the community that is founded through proclamation, unity on the basis of the doctrine that has been proclaimed. This task is designated by the concept of "leadership"; and this leadership consists in the functions of integrating and making manifest the oneness of the community, as the Munich Seminar paper of 1970 described it.[14] The Memorandum (Thesis 12) added the concepts "stimulate" and "coordinate." Responsibility for the unity of the congregation is, as the references to the Augsburg Confession (Art. 28) showed, closely connected with the task of proclamation. This does not rule out the possibility that unordained persons might share in the leadership of the congregation. Still the final responsibility for the unity of the congregation and also for its leadership cannot be separated from the task of proclamation.

The fact that the Memorandum broadens the dominant Protestant understanding of church offices to include responsibility for the unity of the congregation could prove to be significant for the progress of ecumenical discussions on the nature of those offices. Indeed, the function of providing leadership, in the sense of concern for unity, may well be the center of the historic office of bishop and its development since the time of Ignatius of Antioch. In addition, this point of view implies that at every level of the church's life someone must be responsible for unity, and thus there is need for an office of leadership at the local, as well as the regional, and finally also at the worldwide level. This is expressly stated in Thesis 12 of the Memorandum. At every level the same logic holds which is expressed in the words of Roger Schutz which Archbishop Benelli quoted in Augsburg: "If the local congregation needs a pastor to maintain the unity of those who are in danger of being scattered, if each district needs, in the same way, a bishop, a presiding officer, then how can we hope to see the unity of the church restored without a universal shepherd?"[15]

The University Ecumenical Institutes in their Memorandum took the approach that the service of leadership is the comprehensive characteristic of church offices. This broadens the discussion of the understanding of offices to include the questions of the concrete structure of the offices and of their "hierarchical" relationships. Although the questions of the office of the bishop and of papal primacy were not dealt with specifically, the approach to the general concept of church offices through the concept of leadership has far-reaching consequences for the discussion and clarification of these further questions. When this is kept in mind, the verdict of the Commission on Faith of the Conference of German Catholic Bishops appears highly questionable when it says that "the specific Catholic approach was excluded from the Memorandum,"[16] so that it "cannot be regarded as a contribution to the advancement of the ecumenical issue." Gottlob Hild showed greater perception when he observed that the Catholic contributors to the Memorandum "remained throughout the Theses within the framework of Catholic tradition and the accepted Catholic positions."[17] The impression that this was not the case is due primarily to the Memorandum being limited to the general concept of ordination without express discussion and evaluation of the historic office of bishop, the distinction between bishops and presbyters, or the questions involving the primacy of the pope.

This limitation is to be explained by the position that church offices are primarily given to the whole church in all its members and only secondarily differentiated into specific offices of various sorts. In Catholic theology today this is a widely held position, developed especially by Karl Rahner in the framework of his understanding of the church as the original sacrament. It is also found in the decree of the Second Vatican Council on the life and ministry of the priesthood to the extent that the first chapter of this decree starts from the declaration that in Christ "all the faithful are made a holy and royal priesthood." "Hence there is no member who does not have a part in the mission of the whole body" (Art. 2). The transition to the discussion of specific offices is provided by the Pauline idea of differing functions within the body. The relationship between the mission given to the entire body and the variety of functions within the body is also basic to the line of thought followed by the Memorandum. It begins with the task of proclamation, which is entrusted to the entire church (Thesis 6) and from there arrives at the necessity of a variety of functions (Thesis 8). Thesis 9 stresses that the call to discipleship is directed to "the church as a whole," and then as a result to "each individual member for the work to which that member is called through the gift of the Spirit." The explanation of ordination in Thesis 15 comes back to this point, that church offices "involve the mission of the church as a whole and are to be understood as a sharing in the mission of Christ." This line of thought is thus analogous to that of the first chapter of the Decree on the Priesthood of the Second Vatican Council, although it gives greater prominence to the task of proclamation. The only difference is that apostolic succession is not specifically related to the office of bishops, who then give to the priests a share in their official ministry. The reticence of the Memorandum at this point is to be explained not solely as the result of a broader concept of apostolic succession that includes the church in all its members, especially in reference to their faith. It is also to be explained in terms of the idealized view which the Council held of the relationship of apostles, bishops, and priests, and which does not correspond precisely to the historical data. Thesis 10 says, "The distinction between bishops and priests gradually became established." In the light of the difficult historical questions that are to be dealt with here, the Memorandum limited itself to establishing that apostolic succession was a special attribute of the whole church and took on a specific concrete form in the "ministry of leadership." It has already been pointed out that the choice of this concept implies a positive attitude toward the development that led to the formation of the office of bishop in the church, without going into the complicated historical question of the relationship between bishop and presbyter at the church's beginnings.[18]

The nature of leadership in the church in relationship to the participation in Christ's mission that is open to all the faithful is consistently referred to in the Memorandum as "public." The function of leadership "at the local, regional, or universal level" involves, as is explicitly stated, "the public responsibility for the common cause" (Thesis 12). Ordination thus confers "authority" for "the public exercise of responsibility for the one mission of Christ" (Thesis 15). H. Mühlen rightly detected a Protestant element in this view.[19] But it is not simply a product "of Luther's debate with the papal church of his day."[20] It is not primarily polemical in nature, but developed out of the basic question of what constitutes the distinctive characteristic of church offices, in view of the priesthood of all believers and their shared participation in the priesthood of Christ. It is therefore not true that the reference to the public responsibility for the mission of Christ and the apostles, in which all the faithful share, denies that ordination has any special value. Because Mühlen makes this assumption, he can contend that there is an opposition between the "thesis of public responsibility" and the Pauline doctrine of charismatic gifts, because through these gifts the Spirit brings about not only a difference of gifts but "also a difference in content."[21] But the distinctive nature of ordination—that which distinguishes its content from that of other spiritual gifts and ministries—is the authority to exercise public responsibility for that which all Christians share in common. This includes concern for the unity of Christians in their common faith and their common mission. It is precisely this which marks the difference between all other ministries and the special ministry and the special charisma of the offices of the church. Of course the other members of the church also share "in the public nature of the community gathered for worship," but this does not mean that it is their specific public responsibility to be concerned for that which Christians have in common and which unites them all.[22]

What do the critics of the "thesis of the public nature of office" regard as the distinctive nature of church offices? According to Mühlen, "the center of the Catholic understanding of office" consists in the "mediation of salvation through human beings, and in this Christ himself accomplishes the salvation of those being saved."[23] As a result, Mühlen welcomes the statements of the Dombes group, in which the church officer is characterized as the representative of Christ, in contrast to the congregation.[24] L. Scheffczyk also notes the absence in the Memorandum of the idea that the office-bearer represents Christ in contrast to the congregation, and contrasts with it what he regards as the sociological and functional understanding of church offices.[25] In stressing the contrast between the congregation and the church officers as representatives of Christ, both authors are following a view that is traditional in Catholic theology and also the statements of the Second Vatican Council concerning the participation of the church's officers in the threefold office of Christ. There is no need to contradict these statements, even from the Protestant side.[26]

The only question is whether the idea of "representing Christ" is an adequate designation of the distinctive nature of the ordained office. If it is true that all Christians have part in the office and mission of Christ because of their fellowship in

Christ through faith, then it follows, as Luther once wrote, that each Christian should become a Christ for the other (*unusquisque alteri Christus quidam fieri*).[27] This therefore does not constitute any special feature of the ordained office.[28] If representing Christ to the faithful were exclusively ascribed to the ordained office, this would contradict the participation of each believer in the mission of Christ, as affirmed in the statements of the Second Vatican Council. Participation in Christ's mission implies representing Christ for the sake of others. The question must be raised whether the ordained office possesses this function in a distinctive manner that differs from the universal priesthood of believers. There is no doubt that it does. The only issue is what constitutes this distinctive nature and what specific principle this involves. There must be such a principle for the concept of representing Christ, in order to make clear what specific form it takes for the ordained office. According to the Memorandum, the principle of the public nature of the office, the public responsibility for that which involves all the faithful, performs this function. The issue is the participation of the faithful in the mission of Christ (Thesis 15). That which concerns all the faithful in this mission is what the office-bearer stands for in contrast to the faithful (Thesis 7). In this sense, without any misleading, monopolizing associations, we can say that the office-bearer, in contrast to the other members of the church, represents Christ, acts *in persona Christi,* as it is so well expressed, in that he presides over the celebration of the Eucharist. The Memorandum does not use the formula that the office-bearer acts *in persona Christi* in contrast to the other members of the congregation. Its authors might have avoided much criticism if they had made specific use of this formula. But the orthodoxy of an ecumenical text cannot be measured by whether it uses the favorite expressions of one or the other of the participating parties. The authors of the Memorandum had enough confidence in those who would read and evaluate it to believe that they would be able to recognize the matter even in unfamiliar language.

The understanding of church offices that the Memorandum represents combines leadership and its public nature. These two aspects do not simply stand side by side. The distinctive nature and the task of leadership are the result of the public responsibility for the common interest of all, and this sets it off from the role of the other members of the church. To give full expression to this common interest, Christ's truth and his mission, and to do so in contrast to the role of the members of the church, but in the common interest of them all, involves the unity of the church in its faith. In reference to its mission, it also involves the function of leadership. These functions are more specifically expressed as encouragement of the faithful to open themselves to the content of their faith, and in addition as coordination and integration of their differing gifts in the service of their common faith. To this extent, the ordained office represents the common interests of the faith on behalf of the faithful and in respect to those who are outside. It is hard to see how anyone could charge that this description represents a "sociologizing" and "functionalizing" of the offices of the church, as if this would involve a downgrading of the specific Christian content of the office.[29] The demand that the church develop a functional basis for its theory of leadership[30] certainly is not meant in a secular sense, but is directed explicitly toward the functioning of the offices of church leadership in the social context of the life of the church. It is to be understood in a sense that is both "churchly" and "social." The statement adds that the function of leadership is not to be understood "primarily in the sense of consecrating the sacraments." Such a reservation in reference to a sacramentalistic narrowing of the understanding of church offices and a corresponding isolation of the office-bearer in the church's consciousness is certainly not superfluous. Moreover, nothing is said about the coordination of the office with the sacramental life of the church, especially if this is understood in the New Testament concept of the sacred mystery which brings Christ and the church together.

The statements of the Memorandum consciously push the question of the sacramental nature of church office and ordination into the background, because the expression "sacrament" is understood in such a variety of ways in theological language.

Thus it seems appropriate first of all to reach understanding concerning the matter itself, and then to consider whether the concept "sacrament" should be used for it, and if so, in what sense. This is what is meant when Thesis 16 says that such use of terminology is a matter of "linguistic usage." This is a conscious reference to the concept of "doctrinal hermeneutics," which was coined by Karl Rahner.[31] It says first of all that a problem of terminology is involved. According to the degree of latitude accorded to the concept of sacrament, ordination could be included among the sacraments. But it is true that using one terminology or another determines the nature of communication in the church. This is the second factor in "linguistic usage." Whether or how the concept "sacrament" is used is therefore not a matter of indifference, to be left to individual preference. Today, however, the use of the concept of sacrament involves insurmountable difficulties. They arise, not merely because it is possible that there might be broad agreement in the understanding of the activities under consideration—ordination for example—while there was disagreement only over whether to call it a sacrament.[32] More than that, it is difficult today to give a coherent theological basis for any of the interpretations of the concept of sacrament which stood in opposition to each other in the age of the Reformation. Neither the medieval concept of a sacrament, which originated with Augustine, that it is a symbolic action instituted by God, nor the narrower interpretation of the Reformers, which demanded that the concept of sacrament be used only for an action that had been instituted by Jesus himself, can be traced to the Scriptures. To be sure, the Bible used the term *mysterion,* but in a much broader sense. In Eph. 3:4–6 it is used for God's inclusion of the Gentiles in his salvation, and in Col. 1:27 for the unity of Christ and the church in the salvation which God has ordained. These statements are so important that if we wish to use the term "sacrament" today, we ought not to pass over them and restrict the use of the concept to specific institutionalized actions alone. No, our starting point must be the spiritual reality of the church in its fellowship with Christ. In New

Testament terms, this is the mystery of salvation, the content of God's saving plan, which will be revealed in the end time. In this sense the concept of the church as the original sacrament, which has developed in contemporary Catholic theology, is to be accepted, but of course the church is not to be this in itself, but in its fellowship with Christ.[33] Such a comprehensive concept of the sacramental efficacy of the church does not exclude the idea "that the mystery of Christ, which is also the mystery of the church, might be concentrated in an especially meaningful way in specific institutional symbolic actions."[34] It is from this perspective that we should deal with this question of whether the act of ordination could not well be considered a sacrament in that sense, without requiring that the institution of ordination be traceable back to Jesus, as the Protestant position of the sixteenth century demanded.

It seems to me, however, that it is more important to reach an understanding of the meaning of ordination itself than it is to clarify this issue. For such understanding, the most important statement of the Memorandum might be the conclusion of Thesis 17, that for the one ordained, ordination means "the commitment of his whole existence." None of the other specific statements about ordination touch on points in dispute between Lutheran and Catholic theology.[35] In reality these are concentrated around the statement in Thesis 17 that ordination involves "a commitment of the entire existence of the one ordained." This formulation of the issue takes into account the intention of the Catholic doctrine that ordination imparts a sacramental character. It avoids, however, the easily misunderstood and partially misleading secondary implications that have come to be connected with this doctrine, according to which the sacramental character is the basis for a higher state of grace for the one ordained than that enjoyed by the laity. If we exclude such secondary implications, the formula that ordination is a "commitment of the entire existence of the one ordained" meets the central concern of the doctrine of the "sacramental character," and it is thus significant that this formula found acceptance not only from Catholic theologians[36] but also in official Protestant circles, that is, at the Arnoldshain

Conference of the German Lutheran and United Churches in their position paper on the Memorandum, October 1973. The Arnoldshain Conference still could not agree to the conclusion of the Memorandum's Thesis 17, "that the office-bearer is to be ordained only once." The Memorandum concludes, on the basis of "the commitment of one's whole existence," that in analogy to baptism ordination should be performed only once. The Arnoldshain Conference maintained, to the contrary, that it seems that "the essence of ordination as the commitment of the entire being of the one ordained is not abandoned if the church, in the instance of a new commission after the expiration of an earlier task, were to perform a new ordination." The key point in the formulation of the Memorandum, however, is that ordination as a "commitment of one's whole existence" has, in contrast to all limited commissioning, which corresponds to investiture in a specific office, an unlimited and unconditional nature. Thus in the Memorandum (Thesis 22d) a clear distinction is drawn between ordination and investiture. The position taken by the Arnoldshain Conference on this point shows, as it shows elsewhere with its doubt concerning the indispensable nature of the laying on of hands, something of the difficulty which the theological consensus of the six ecumenical institutes still encounters even on the Protestant side. Agreement among Protestants on the question of the unrepeatable nature of ordination and on the related distinction between ordination and investiture will have especial significance for the continuation of ecumenical discussion on church offices. This makes the positive reception of the formula that ordination is a commitment of the whole of one's existence all the more important. It could prove to be the starting point for the necessary process of clarification.

Did the Memorandum of the six university institutes achieve ecumenical agreement on the mutual recognition of church offices? The Memorandum represents agreement among the six institutes on the theological presuppositions for such an act of recognition, nothing more, but also nothing less. Not only on the Catholic side, but on the Protestant side as well, there are in this connection a great many positions on theology and church polity that still stand in the way of such agreement. For these positions the Memorandum can constitute a challenge, and its purpose will have been fulfilled if it contributes to a further clarification of the question in theological discussion and also in the official deliberations of the church, as was the wish of the Arnoldshain Conference.

8
The Lord's Supper—
Sacrament of Unity

Throughout Christianity there is an awareness today that the denominational disagreements of the past are no longer relevant. In the light of contemporary experience and in the face of the tasks that confront all Christians in today's world it seems possible, even inevitable, that we will achieve a new understanding of the Christian faith unencumbered by controversies inherited from the past. In many gatherings, Christians from differing denominational traditions experience a new sense of community. Ecumenism has long since moved past the stage at which ecumenical contacts were primarily the concern of theologians and church officials. An ecumenical awareness brings more and more changes in the thinking of local congregations. The movement toward Christian unity, which is widely regarded as a condition for a believable Christian witness, has become one of the most important expressions of Christian life in our day.

This is often accompanied in many places by impatience and dissatisfaction with the present status of the churches and with the often disappointing slowness with which they move toward a new unity of Christianity. There may be good reasons for avoiding undue haste, which might secure the illusion of unity at the price of a sense of community in our understanding of the faith and thus lead to new divisions. It is still true, however, that there has often been more progress toward unity in the everyday life of ordinary Christians than in the official church bodies. This uneven progress has in itself a positive significance for the progress toward unity, because the progressive development of ecumenical forms of life in the congregations and in ecumenical groups make it possible for the leaders of the church to set their sights on continuing developments involving the entire church.

All this is widely recognized by the leaders of the churches. Yet there are both Catholic and Protestant leaders who feel concern or even react negatively when ecumenical groups that have attained an advanced awareness of Christian community seek to express this experience in common celebrations of the Eucharist. This happens because, in terms of traditional concepts and practice, fellowship at the Lord's Supper is the expression and confirmation of full ecclesiastical fellowship, including unity of doctrine as well as mutual recognition of church officers. Since these prerequisites are still not present in the relationship between Catholics and Protestants, and also between many Protestant churches, joint celebrations of the Lord's Supper are regarded today by many responsible theologians and church officers as an unjustified and illusory anticipation of a unity that has not yet been achieved.

Skepticism concerning a eucharistic fellowship which many think is premature presupposes—and in this it is correct—that celebration of the Eucharist is a sign of the full community of faith within the church of Christ. But the unity of Christians which already exists in the church has its basis in the unity of the faithful with Christ. "The bread which we break, is it not a participation in the body of Christ? Because there is one bread, we who are many are one body, for we all partake of the one bread" (I Cor. 10:16b–17). Fellowship with Christ through participation in his body is the basis for the fellowship of Christians in the body of Christ. Therefore the Eucharist is not only the expression and sign of an already existing church unity. It is also the source and root by which Christian unity lives and is constantly being renewed. This supports the view that fellowship at the Lord's table is not merely the goal of the process of church union but that it can also be the present power of Christ by which we travel the path toward that goal.

It is also significant that the celebration of the Eucharist is not only directed toward the past, in that it contemplates the death of Christ, but that it is also a sign of hope. The New Testament accounts of the Last Supper express clearly its relationship to that future fellowship around the table in the Kingdom of God. In the history of the doctrine of the Lord's Supper too little account has been taken of this, as is almost universally recognized today. But if in the Eucharist we are already celebrating the future fellowship in the Kingdom of God, and if the community gathered for the Lord's Supper is looking forward to the return of its one Lord, is it not then also possible that the unity of the church can be found in the Eucharist in the form of hope and not only as a unity that has already been achieved? Is it not then possible that in our celebration of Christ's last supper our shared hope in him can also establish and strengthen our present fellowship? A study document of the Commission on Faith and Order of the World Council of Churches published in 1969 says: "In the Eucharist the church thinks not only of the redeeming death of Christ under Pontius Pilate; it also looks toward the final consummation of the Kingdom of God and knows at every time and in every place, as it knew during the lifetime of Jesus, a foretaste of this reality. . . . This foretaste of the Kingdom of God calls humanity to reconciliation and to a new life. Through its dynamic of creative anticipation it overcomes human fears about the future and frees men and women to act courageously amidst constant change, in order to build a more truly human society." Thus the central Christian meaning of the Eucharist, and with it the understanding of what is sacramental, can be experienced in a new way by a Christianity that is still under way toward its final unity and toward the unity of all mankind.

The decisive point of view for the discussion of fellowship in the Lord's Supper might be that it is Jesus Christ himself who is the one who invites us to come to his table and thus to take part in the fellowship of his body. This invitation is directed to Jesus' disciples, but it also contains something of the lack of reserve and the openness of Jesus' practice in his fellowship at table with tax collectors and sinners, who were united with him through such fellowship and thereby obtained a share in the hope for the coming Kingdom of God. Does the church have a right to narrow the scope of Jesus' invitation by supplementary conditions for participation in the supper of our Lord? A statement made by American Jesuit theologians in 1969 concerning the Lord's Supper says that the church is "the administrator of the sacraments, but not their Lord; the Lord of the sacraments, Lord of the sacred table, as the one who invites, distributes, institutes, is Jesus Christ. He is Lord also of the church and of the churches, standing beyond their differences and already overcoming their separation in himself." In keeping with the table fellowship which the earthly Jesus observed, the churches and their priests will not exclude from participation in the Lord's Supper anyone who comes with the sincere intention of taking part in the meal offered by Jesus Christ, at least not as long as they understand their ministry of the sacrament at the altar as service in accordance with the will of Jesus when he instituted the meal. The only criterion that the liturgist needs in deciding whom to admit is whether those who come have a sincere intention to participate, or whether a known situation makes it impossible to assume that those who come do so with a sincere will to be in fellowship with Jesus through the meal which he instituted. It is in this light that every restriction on admission to the Lord's Supper, including limiting it to baptized Christians, must be justified and shown to have a right to exist.

Denominational Differences in the Doctrine of the Lord's Supper

In the past, many churches regarded denominational differences in the doctrine of the Lord's Supper as hindrances to admission to the Supper, and even today such doctrinal differences are advanced as the reason why it is not possible to have Eucharist fellowship between Protestants and Catholics. The first thing to be said in this connection is that in recent years the traditional distinctions involving the nature of the Mass as a sacrifice and the transubstantiation of the elements have lost much of their force. Second, the significance of doctrinal questions and distinctions for the life of faith and for the administration of the sacraments is to be judged in a manner quite different from that of earlier periods in church history. On the first point, a study document of the Commission on Faith and Order has commented on recent theological explorations into the questions of the real presence of Christ, of the eucharistic sacrifice, and of the meaning of epiclesis for the Eucharist celebration. It states: "The growing unity in this area astonishes many who have had no knowledge of theological developments." The opposition of the churches of the Reformation to the doctrine of transubstantiation has been made largely irrelevant today by the introduction of the idea of a transformation in meaning (transignification), which is to be seen as marking a change in the nature of the issue. On the other side, Catholic theology has recently dealt with the Reformation approach that regarding the Mass as a sacrifice makes it in some way a repetition of the once-for-all sacrifice of Christ and thus destroys the uniqueness of that sacrifice. This has been dealt with in a convincing manner by stressing that the eucharistic liturgy is the sacramental representation of the work accomplished once and for all by Christ. Since participation through faith in Christ and in all that belongs to Christ is a central motif of the Protestant understanding of faith, it will be difficult for Protestants to deny at this point that this participation can also be extended to the meaning of the death of Christ as sacrifice—at least to the degree to which the death of Christ has this significance. In any case, throughout the entire Latin tradition we cannot fail to recognize a certain one-sided overemphasis on the nature of the death of Christ as a sacrifice in the sense of an accomplishment by which Jesus reconciles a wrathful God. That is another question, a difference of theologies, but scarcely enough of a difference to divide churches from one another, especially since theologians in the Reformation tradition have also frequently held this understanding of the sacrifice of Jesus.

There is increasing agreement today that the existence of a multiplicity of theological formulations, even of conflicting ones, does not always exclude the possibility of unity in the faith. For example, the theological disagreements of the age of the Reformation were so thoroughly conditioned by differing perspectives and by different modes of theological language that it is hard to decide where the theologians were simply talking past each other and where deeper disagreements were involved. Insight into such limitations of theological perspective should not reduce theologians to despair. On the contrary, it can lead to a new estimate of the Christian conviction that the reality of the life of faith and especially of the eucharistic participation in Christ cannot be fully realized through theological reflection. In the past the significance with theological formulas have for faith was often overestimated. It may well be one of the most important theological tasks of the present day to correct this mistaken emphasis, and to do so through a different type of theological knowledge, not through a renunciation of theology. What is involved can be seen more clearly in the devotional life centering around the Eucharist than anywhere else in the life of the church. Everyone who takes part in Christ's meal enters into a fellowship—with Jesus as well as with all others who take part in this meal—the reality of which far exceeds human comprehension. Thus participation in the fellowship of the Lord's Supper by Christians from differing denominational traditions can make us aware of this with especial clarity. On the other hand, such experience can make us more clearly aware of the community we have experienced even in our understanding of the faith.

The problem of church offices remains. Since according to the traditional Catholic view only a legitimately consecrated priest can administer the Eucharist in a valid manner, it has been denied that Protestant churches have—as many of them believe they have—the actual presence of Christ in their celebrations of the Lord's Supper, and that those who commune are actually united with him. On the Protestant side, it is not denied that Christ is really present in the Roman Mass and is received by the faithful. At the Second Vatican Council, Catholic rejection of the Protestant Lord's Supper gave way to a limited recognition. Thus began a development that still continues. If the ecclesiastical status of the Protestant churches is no longer rejected out of hand, this has consequences for the evaluation of church offices in these churches.

Mutual Recognition of Church Offices

There is no great distance between the Protestant basis of church offices in terms of the priesthood of all baptized believers and the concept that is gaining ground in Catholic theology that the church office, a continuation of the apostolic mission, is initially given to the church as a whole and only then distributed among individual offices. The positions are especially close, since Protestants do not need to insist that the office which exercises authority publicly is identical with the priesthood of all believers. Moreover, the Protestant churches believe that they are in the succession of the apostles and of the apostolic mission, a mission that includes the task of proclamation as well as that of leading the congregation. Thus there seems to be no reason why in principle it is not possible to enter into a process of progressive mutual recognition of the church's offices on both sides. In this process it would naturally be impossible to avoid the question of a supreme office in Christianity, but it would not be necessary to agree on a specific understanding of such an office.

The consequence for eucharistic fellowship is that an official and regular concelebration of the Eucharist by Protestant and Catholic clergy, using a liturgy that would not be merely tolerated by one of the churches but would have the full approval of both, will be possible only at a quite advanced stage of the process of mutual recognition of the churches. By contrast, so-called open communion, the admission of the members of other churches to the celebration of the Lord's Supper in one's own church, is already appropriate at the present stage of interchurch relations. It corresponds to the invitation of the one Lord to all his disciples, which is to be honored by each church in its own forms of worship, and nothing stands in its way, because in our present situation the claims of members of other churches to be disciples of Jesus is no longer denied. Even today open communion is practiced to a limited extent and tolerated by the churches.

The next step would be official agreement among the churches concerning mutual open communion, involving general permission for the members of each church to take part in the celebration of the Lord's Supper in the other churches. Such agreement, which already exists among the Protestant churches of Germany, can no longer be regarded as unattainable by Protestants and Catholics, especially since it does not need to involve the recognition of the Eucharist celebration of the other church as equally valid in every respect. Indeed, there are already ecumenical groups and entire congregations who join in celebration of the Eucharist, with participation by clergy from both sides. This naturally raises the problem of a common liturgy, which might be solved by modifying existing forms or by using a more or less free liturgy. Such common eucharistic celebrations with a common liturgy are clearly irregular. They exist in anticipation of a stage at which ecumenical developments converge, but which the churches as a whole have not yet reached. Even so, such celebrations should not be regarded as a breach of a member's solidarity with his or her own church.

The unity of Christians through their participation in faith in their one Lord is here seeking expression in an irregular form not yet generally accepted, but it is the principle by which each of the existing churches lives. Therefore such celebrations, insofar as they exhibit a truly Christian intention, should be permitted by the churches. They should be seen as a sign of the future of the one Lord, which is the concern of all Christians. The Lord desires the unity of all his disciples, and he is present in every celebration of the Lord's Supper, in order to unite in him all who believe.

9
A Protestant View
of the Doctrine
of the Lord's Supper

*A Contribution to Ecumenical Discussion on the
Lord's Supper*

As has happened in other areas of theology, the traditional denominational debates about the Lord's Supper, or Eucharist, have lost much of their sharpness. This can be regarded as due primarily to the effect of historical consciousness. Today it is not possible for theology to ignore the problems resulting from the historical distance between the classical dogmatic formulations and the statements of the early church on the one hand and from our contemporary experience of reality on the other. In the doctrine of the Lord's Supper these problems confront us with especial clarity. The Lord's Supper is dependent, as is no other aspect of church life, on its being instituted by the historical Jesus, and it is therefore particularly vulnerable to historical criticism. Exegetical research has shown much disparity of motifs in the New Testament texts dealing with the Lord's Supper and is still far from a unanimous or even converging verdict even on fundamental points. As a result, everyone who expects the Scripture to provide an answer or at least a reliable indication of the meaning and origins of the Lord's Supper feels increasingly discouraged and bewildered by the state of exegetical discussion. There is nothing even resembling a consensus concerning the original form of the earliest celebrations of the Lord's Supper or on the question of whether it originated with Jesus himself. This creates a highly difficult situation for the task of constructing a theological doctrine of the Lord's Supper, because the institution of the Supper by Jesus is not a factor that has only external significance and could be neglected as far as the content and essence of the Supper are concerned. On the contrary, according to the view of all Christians it is of central significance for the nature of the Eucharist itself.

I

The difficulty of the historical problems involved in the transmission of the Lord's Supper could make it attractive to attempt a systematic approach to the doctrine of the Eucharist independent of exegetical and historical questions. The most likely point of departure would be the general concept of sacrament. Actually, since the days of high scholasticism the Lord's Supper has been discussed in the framework of the doctrine of the sacraments. Protestant theology too has usually taken the doctrine of the means of grace as its starting point, discussing the relationship of word and sacrament in general, before dealing specifically with the sacraments retained by the churches of the Reformation—baptism and the Lord's Supper. Paul Althaus[37] represents a continuation of this approach in the theological work of the present century. In the Protestant theological literature of the present day, however, it is over-whelmingly the case that the concept of sacrament is treated in a summary of the institutions of baptism and Lord's Supper, which are regarded as needing their own theological basis. This was also the approach of the Augsburg Confession, where, in contrast to the Schwabach Articles, it is only after the discussion of baptism (Art. 9), the Lord's Supper (Art. 10), and also confession and penance (Arts. 11 and 12), that the concept of sacrament is discussed as a "sign" of "God's intention toward us." Werner Elert, who at the beginning of his chapter on the Lord's Supper discusses the concept of sacrament, energetically opposes taking a general concept of sacrament as the starting point for the discussion of baptism and the Lord's Supper, because by doing so, "the contingency of the facts" of these two liturgical procedures would not receive their proper due.[38] After all, would it not be appropri-ate to decide first through a general concept of sacrament "what meaning such acts as baptism and Lord's Supper could have on the basis of the gospel as understood by Reformation thought."[39] No, not merely the Protestant doctrine of Scripture but the conviction that Jesus himself instituted the Lord's Supper calls on us to begin with the question of the distinctive nature of its original form and meaning. This logic forced on us by the data will not permit us to avoid the difficult exegetical and historical problems involved.

There is an advantage to be gained from the decision not to delay discussion of the Lord's Supper until general observations have been made on the means of grace and the relationship of word and sacrament. It frees the discussions of the Lord's Supper from controversies over the number of sacraments and their nature in general. It is important for ecumenical discussions to be clear on this point: the concept of sacrament in the technical sense as a comprehensive designation of a class of church rites rests on reflection concerning the individual rites, and emphasizes that which they have in common. It is then no longer of decisive importance whether this concept of sacrament is conceived in broader or narrower terms, and whether on that basis a larger or smaller number of sacraments is agreed upon.

Reformation doctrine held that it was correct to take a narrow view of the concept of sacrament. The probable reason for this is that the Reformers, with their orientation to the word of God, were opposed to any dogmatizing of human traditions in the church. Only such rites as Christ himself had instituted could be regarded as signs of the divine will for us, and thus as sacraments. But precisely at this point a further and final argument presents itself to our contemporary way of thinking, in opposition to any basing of the doctrine of the Lord's Supper on a general concept of sacrament. The distinction between the earthly Jesus and the Exalted One, whose words and instructions cannot so readily be separated from the formation of the traditions of the Christian community, is more obvious to present-day exegetes than it was to those of the Reformation age. Therefore, in reference to the Lord's Supper and baptism it is no longer possible to speak in the same sense of their being instituted by Jesus. Nowhere in the Christian tradition is baptism as a church rite traced back to a command of the earthly Jesus. According to the earliest Christian tradition, it was a command of the risen Christ that authorized the church to administer baptism, even though the performance of baptism without doubt took place as a continuation in the Christian church of John's baptism, in remembrance of the fact that Jesus himself had permitted John to baptize him. Even the institution of the Lord's Supper by the earthly Jesus is disputed, especially as far as the command to repeat it is concerned. But in the case of the Lord's Supper, and only here, it is at least possible to discuss whether it was instituted by Jesus in distinction from a later development in the church. In contrast to baptism, the earliest Christian traditions concerning the Lord's Supper consistently trace it back to the earthly Jesus himself, and the unanimity of the tradition at this point should be rejected only if weighty arguments of historical criticism force us to do so. The concept of institution by Jesus, which the Reformers took as their decisive criterion for their general concept of sacrament and for limiting it to baptism and Lord's Supper, appears to us today as a specific point in the problem of understanding the Lord's Supper.

II

Before we can clarify the question of whether it is historically justified to speak of an "institution" of the Lord's Supper by Jesus, we must first clarify the meaning of this expression. Some theologians, including Elert, think we can speak of the institution of the Lord's Supper by Jesus only if the last supper of Jesus actually took place on Maundy Thursday evening in the form reported in the Synoptic Gospels, and also the command to repeat the observance, as transmitted by Paul, can be traced back to Jesus and represents his direct command.[40] On the other hand, for Paul Althaus the idea of institution does not depend on an explicit command to repeat the Lord's Supper, which he held to have been supplied by Paul. It is enough for him that "the saying concerning repeated observances is based on the meaning of Jesus' last supper," and "to that extent in reality goes back to Jesus."[41] Althaus even went a step farther. He said that he was prepared to speak of an institution "not by Jesus, to be sure, but by the living Christ" even if the origin of the eucharistic tradition lay entirely in the period after Easter."[42] But certain objections necessarily arise. An institution of the Eucharist by the risen Lord would of course correspond to the institution of baptism, as it is reported by Matthew, but that would not be identical with that institution which is reported in all the New Testament texts that pertain to the Lord's Supper, because they all place it in the period before Easter.

At this point the wording of the first of the Arnoldshain Theses is remarkably imprecise. It says, "The Supper which we celebrate is based on the institution and command of Jesus Christ, the Lord who for us was delivered over to death and rose again." Helmut Gollwitzer says in his commentary on this thesis that the wording was designated to avoid the question of the historicity and the content of the Last Supper. By speaking of institution by Christ, the statement on confessions means "not a historical judgment, but—as in all our listening to the New Testament—the assurance that through the witness of the community we hear the command and promise of the Lord of the church in his unity as the one who is both earthly and exalted."[43] However beautiful and full of theology this explanation sounds, the question remains of what this "assurance" is based on, especially in reference to the observation about the unity of the exalted with the earthly Jesus in connection with the origin of the Lord's Supper. The belief that this origin involves the earthly Jesus is not something that we can simply dispense with, if we are to speak of an institution of the Supper by Christ in a sense that is true to the earliest Christian traditions of the Lord's Supper. In that case, the historical question can hardly be avoided, as Gollwitzer thinks. Peter Brunner has rightly accused the first Arnoldshain thesis at this point as attesting to a "certain theological weakness," because it does not mention the night of betrayal as the situation in which the Lord's Supper originated. On the other hand, the difficulties involved in the question of the historicity of Jesus' Last Supper cannot be dogmatically passed by. Dogmatic theology will do well to frame the concept of the institution of the Lord's Supper by Jesus broadly enough that the unsolved historical questions about its origin will not be prejudged, but will remain open. We will not, however, be able to give up the continuity between the early Christian Eucharist and Jesus, in which it is understood as a historical development of a central core inaugurated by Jesus himself, unless we are willing to abandon the conviction that the Lord's Supper was instituted by Jesus.

III

It is possible to establish a connection between the earthly career of Jesus and the earliest Christian traditions of the Lord's Supper and its practice, a connection which permits us to speak of Jesus' having instituted the Lord's Supper but which does not build on the events of the Last Supper itself or involve us in the disputes over its historicity. Ernst Lohmeyer has pointed out the connections between the eucharistic tradition and the daily meals of Jesus, which he shared not only with his disciples but with "tax collectors and sinners." He also pointed out a connection with the idea of an eschato-logical meal as a metaphor of future salvation in the Kingdom of God. This idea has been taken up by other scholars, even by some such as Eduard Schweizer and Willi Marxsen, who are skeptical about the traditions of the Last Supper. Just as the future Kingdom of God was already present in the words and deeds of Jesus, so too in Jesus' fellowship at meals with his disciples—but also with "tax collectors and sinners"—there is already an anticipation of the joyous eschatological feast in the Kingdom of God.

The authors of the Arnoldshain Theses also had in mind the connection between the Lord's Supper and the early Christian eucharistic celebrations on the one hand and Jesus' custom of shared meals on the other. Thus for Gollwitzer as well, the establishment of the Lord's Supper is a "present invitation to table fellowship in continuation with the fellowship with the disciples, tax collectors, and sinners (Lohmeyer), but as a present invitation it is given by the risen Lord, who has entered into his Kingdom, and is thus an invitation to table fellowship in the Kingdom of God" (p. 25). To be sure,

Gollwitzer makes a distinction between the institution of the Lord's Supper as "continuation" and the table fellowship of Jesus that preceded it. Thus, in a strange manner the institution of the Lord's Supper is connected with the exaltation of Jesus, in contrast to the intention of the New Testament accounts, which ascribe its institution to the earthly Jesus. Moreover, Jesus' invitation is not primarily an invitation to "table fellowship in the Kingdom of God" in the sense of an "invitation of the exalted Lord," but is, beyond doubt, related primarily to the meals of Jesus' earthly life. Of course firm belief in Jesus' resurrection and exaltation was not without influence on the practice of the early Christian Eucharist and on the meaning ascribed to it. Now the meal instituted by Jesus was celebrated as fellowship with the One who had been crucified, who had risen, and who was coming again. This does not alter in the least the belief found in all the earliest Christian traditions that the institution of the meal goes back to the time of the earthly work of the Lord, who is now exalted at the right hand of God. If this starting point is not regarded as limited to the account of Jesus' last supper, but is seen in connection with his entire practice of shared meals in the time before Easter, then it is possible to agree with Peter Brunner that "even the fellowship at table with his disciples before the last night instituted the practice,"[44] instead of joining Gollwitzer in ascribing it to the risen Lord. The Arnoldshain Theses failed to express the connection between Jesus' last supper as reported in the tradition and his practice at meals before Easter in a way that would prove fruitful for the theological concept of the institution of the Supper. If they had done this, the historical difficulties in the question of the antecedents of Jesus' last evening before his arrest would have been taken into account, without emptying the theological idea of institution of the Eucharist of its content, as the text of the Theses has done.

As far as the evidence preserved in the tradition allows us to determine, the implicit meaning of the pre-Easter table fellowship of Jesus corresponds to a very large extent with what the New Testament accounts present as the explicit meaning of the Last Supper. Just as confessing faith in Jesus and his message guarantees participation in the future Kingdom of

God and indeed confers it now (to the extent that the lordship of God has already begun in the coming of Jesus and in his work), so too table fellowship with Jesus guarantees and confers participation in the joyous meal of the coming Kingdom. The words of explanation of the Last Supper as they have come down to us, especially the words over the bread, express this meaning. What we share in Jesus, mediated by our sharing at his table, guarantees "even now participation in the future fellowship of the Kingdom of God," as the first Arnold-shain thesis states, and thus articulates a significant new point of view in the history of the Protestant doctrine of the Lord's Supper.[45]

The words of interpretation in the accounts of the Last Supper go beyond these basic thoughts, especially in pointing out a connection between the death of Jesus and what he did at the Supper. This is especially true in the form of the eschatological statement (Mark 14:25 and pars.), in the atonement motif of the *hyper* formula (Mark 14:24c and pars.; I Cor. 11:24b), and in the Pauline "remembrance" motif (I Cor. 11:25b), and finally in the connection between the new covenant and the blood of Jesus, where the emphasis is placed somewhat differently in Paul and Mark. There is dispute about the originality of all these motifs. The fewest objections are raised to the eschatological words. The *hyper* formula arouses reservations, because it is clearly bound neither to the words over the bread nor to those over the cup, but in Mark with the cup and in Paul with the bread. A secondary omission in one place or the other is unlikely, if we assume that the atonement motif belonged to the original wording, whether that of the bread or that of the cup. Even the words over the cup that speak of a (new) covenant through the blood of Jesus have been regarded as secondary. Moreover, scholars have viewed critically the inclusion of the account of institution in the framework of a Passover meal, which is how we find it in the Synoptic Gospels, but which contradicts the Johannine account of the Passion.

Still it is only the eschatological elements that tell us that Jesus himself drew a connection between table fellowship and his death, and that the atonement motif, the interpretation of

his death as a covenant sacrifice, and the typological relationship to the Passover must be regarded as an integral development of the distinctive meaning of the death of Jesus, which is
shared by those who through the meal have fellowship with
Jesus himself. It then becomes a matter of lesser importance
whether Jesus himself formulated explicitly one or the other
interpretation of his approaching death. The decisive factor is
still that the invitation to table fellowship with him and the
participation in future salvation which this includes (in the
meaning of the Lutheran tradition's emphasis on the element
of "promise") go back to Jesus himself, and also that fellowship with him at table brings with it participation in the saving
significance of his death. A further factor that is basic for the
question of whether Jesus at least implicitly instituted the
Eucharist celebrated by the post-Easter community is the
universal nature of the invitation, beyond the then-existing
circle of disciples. This universality of Jesus' invitation to table
fellowship is documented in the practice of the historic Jesus
of eating with "tax collectors and sinners," and is reinforced
by the universal significance, established on other bases, of his
death for our salvation. Thus it seems to be justifiable to speak
of an institution of the Lord's Supper, but to evaluate it in the
total context of Jesus' activity in the period before Easter, and
especially that of his practice of sharing his daily meals.

IV

An understanding of the Lord's Supper oriented to the
results of exegetical and historical research must inevitably
lead today to basic changes in our perspective on the traditional doctrinal statements and also on the questions raised in the
debates that preceded these statements. Such changes will
affect every type of denominational doctrine. As a result, the
discussion can no longer move on the tracks of traditional
doctrinal controversy. More important, all Christian denominations are challenged by the theme of the Lord's Supper to
rethink the real meaning of the Eucharist. This constitutes the
ecumenical challenge of the difficult exegetical situation involved in this question.

The debates out of which the dogma of transubstantiation developed, and later both the Lutheran doctrine and the Reformed doctrine of the Lord's Supper, must be judged today as manifesting an all too one-sided interest in the so-called elements. Augustine's definition of a sacrament (*accedit verbum ad elementum, et fit sacramentum,* "the word is added to the element and makes it a sacrament") made it easy for the entire Latin history of doctrine to restrict the meaning in this manner, but we can observe as early as Mark's formulation of the words over the cup a shifting of accent away from personal fellowship with Jesus to participation in his body and blood—as Ignatius of Antioch expressed it in classic form (To the Ephesians 20:2)—the *pharmakon athanasias,* the medicine of immortality. This could happen because it was forgotten that the word over the bread in its putative Aramaic original form *(guph)* did not refer to the body of Jesus in its material quality as such, but to Jesus himself, and that the word over the cup in the form transmitted by Paul points to the new covenant founded by the death of Jesus and not directly to the drinking of the blood of Jesus, a procedure that would have been unacceptable to Jews.

On the other hand, recent discussion of the Lord's Supper, by Catholics as well as by Protestants,[46] reveals a concern to give a more central place to the personal character of our participation in Jesus through the Lord's Supper. And when it is stressed that the person of Jesus as the content of that which is given in the Lord's Supper is not "a disembodied, purely spiritual being," not a "personal self separated from his body that hung on the cross and from the blood that was shed there,"[47] this is merely expressing the identity of self and body that is contained in what is assumed to be the original Aramaic content of the word over the bread. The fourth Arnoldshain thesis emphasized this meaning of the personal character of that which is given in the Lord's Supper, its identity with the person of Jesus himself. And the fifth thesis formulated the relevant safeguards against both an abstract spiritual understanding of the Lord's Supper and an abstract material understanding, in the sense of a natural or supernatural substance. It remains only to add that it is not the isolated person of Jesus that is the gift of salvation which we come to share in the Lord's Supper. The gift must be recognized and accepted in the person of Jesus in his concrete reality, that is, in his relation to the coming Kingdom of God, for the sake of which Jesus came into the world. Our share in God's future salvation is guaranteed by the fellowship we have with Jesus, the messenger of that salvation. That is the full concept of the gift of salvation that is involved in the Lord's Supper. The Arnoldshain Theses gave clear expression to this eschatological dimension in the first thesis. But in the fourth thesis, which is decisive for the understanding of the salvation given in the Lord's Supper, it is not mentioned. The emphasis there is entirely on the personal interpretation of participation in the body and blood of Christ. As a consequence, the relationship between participation in Christ and participation in the salvation of the coming Kingdom of God is not adequately clarified in the theses.

If the personal meaning of our participation in Jesus guaranteed through the Lord's Supper demands a de-emphasis on the one-sided concentration on the "elements" in our understanding of the Supper and what it gives to us, then the isolation of the gift from the personal event of the celebration of the Eucharist must be overcome. Toward this goal the Arnoldshain Theses have stressed the ecclesiological significance of the Lord's Supper as the basis of the fellowship in the body of Christ among those who receive the gift of Jesus, and by so doing they have reclaimed a central element of meaning in the tradition of the Lord's Supper which has often been neglected in Protestant discussions, but was of central significance for the early Christian community.

V

The tradition's one-sided emphasis on what happens to the elements may be connected with the interpretation of the presence of Christ in the event of the Eucharist from earliest times in terms of an epiphany, a descent of the bodily nature of the exalted Lord in the bread and wine on the altar. His presence was not always understood as being mediated through the remembrance of the crucified One, remembrance of the historical Jesus. Of course no denominational expression of the doctrine of the Lord's Supper forgot that the exalted Lord was identical with the One who died on the cross. In this sense the remembrance of Jesus' death had its place not only in the eucharistic liturgy but also in theological reflection. But the question of the presence of Jesus in the Eucharist was not dealt with primarily as the question of how the one participating in the celebration shared in the historical Jesus and in the event of his death on the cross. In terms of salvation, interest in this question was directly tied to participation in the transfigured being of the exalted Lord. Consequently his presence was not thought of as mediated through participation in the historical Jesus and his cross but as his unmediated presence, descended from heaven, present in the elements.

It must be said that the Catholic doctrine of the Eucharist as a sacrifice gave clearer expression in its own way to the connection of the celebration of the Lord's Supper with the One who died on the cross than did the Protestant interpretations. As the result of their criticism of the concept of sacrifice, Protestants were inclined to see what is given in the Supper as only the *fruit* of the sacrifice on the cross, the application of what was achieved there, but no longer the presence of the crucified Lord himself. On the other hand, the idea of a liturgical reenactment of the sacrifice on the cross does not in itself exclude the possibility of understanding it as a representative repetition, and even a supplementation of what occurred once and for all in the death of Jesus. In addition to motifs that developed in the history of the liturgy,[48] such interpretations were aided by the concept of the presence of the Lord in the Eucharist as an epiphany of the exalted Lord on the altar, by analogy to and parallel with the event of the incarnation. This was true especially when it was combined with an understanding of the Eucharist as the reenactment of Jesus' death on the cross. Thus Odo Casel's new formulation of the idea of reenactment has made a contribution by conceiving of Christ's presence in the Eucharist as the presence of the crucified One himself, and only so as the presence of the exalted Lord. Consequently it is possible to give a convincing answer to the Protestant suspicion that the eucharistic sacrifice involved in some way a repetition and supplementation of the once-for-all sacrifice of Christ on Golgotha. Even so, the concept of sacrifice in the interpretation of the Eucharist, together with the one-sided concentration on the elements and the equally one-sided understanding of the presence of Christ in the Eucharist as the exalted Lord, constitutes a third aspect of the narrowing of the doctrine of the Eucharist in contrast to its origins in the Lord's Supper. The consequences of this narrowing are by no means to be found only in Catholic doctrine but are present in Protestant doctrine as well.

VI

It is well known that it is not the doctrine of transubstantiation that constitutes the real contrast between the Lutheran and the Catholic interpretation of the Lord's Supper, but the understanding of the Eucharist as a sacrifice which the church offers, which is not merely a sacrifice of thanksgiving but a sacrifice of atonement. In his criticism of the Roman Mass, Luther attacked primarily the concept (which he believed was expressed not only in theology but also in the liturgy of the Mass) that Christ's sacrifice could be capable of and in need of any supplementation. Because of this claim, Luther felt that the sacrifice of the Mass belonged to works righteousness and might even be its most blatant expression.

It can scarcely be denied that in the sixteenth century there was reason for such criticism, if not of the liturgy of the Mass itself, then at least of its contemporary theological interpretation. But that need not detain us here. The present-day Catholic doctrine of the Eucharist and the eucharistic sacrifice in its totality is in any case no longer subject to such criticisms or questioning,[49] even though now and then concepts are encountered which are close to the idea that the sacrifice of Christ is supplemented by its reenactment in the sacrifice of the Mass.[50] The idea of reenactment, which has been developed by Catholic theologians since Odo Casel, clearly goes beyond a mere application of the effects of the once-for-all event of atonement. It connotes, rather, that this event itself is made present in the cultic procedure. This does not necessarily involve the idea of repetition or supplementation. On the contrary, such an interpretation is excluded by the sacrifice on the cross. A repetitive reenactment is not repetition on the plane of a historically unique event.

Neither does this change anything in the understanding of the eucharistic sacrifice as atonement. If the cross of Christ was an atoning sacrifice, and if in the Eucharist the historic atonement is present, not merely an exalted bodily nature of Christ, then the celebration of the Eucharist is sacramental participation in Christ's atoning sacrifice, insofar as reconciliation is correctly described as atonement. This is a point to which we must return. Here I only want to stress that Protestant distrust of the understanding of the Lord's Supper as expiation is without basis if that involves only the real presence of the crucified Christ, under the condition that the cross of Christ is correctly understood as an expiatory sacrifice. At this point there is no justification for lapsing back into the old attacks on the Roman Catholic theology of the Lord's Supper and appealing to the concepts of "application" and thank offering.[51] Such limitations are significant if we are expressing what the worship offered at the Lord's Supper can mean in itself, but not in understanding the real presence of Christ in the Eucharist. Much more light is cast on the subject by E. Iserloh's statement that the Mass is "an expiatory sacrifice, not in spite of, but because of its unity with the sacrifice offered at Golgotha."[52] This position must always be based on the assumption that Jesus' path to the cross is truly to be understood as an expiation. In this Christological assumption the Reformers were in complete agreement with the dominant concept in the Latin church; their only concern was to stress the total adequacy of Christ's sacrifice. In terms of these presuppositions, their rejection of the concept of the sacrament of the Mass as an expiatory sacrifice is to be explained, first of all, as resistance to the idea that there could be sacramental presentations of sacrifice to supplement the sacrifice of Christ. Second, they wanted to stress that Christ's presence was to be thought of as the presence of the exalted

Christ, but not that of the historical Jesus or as reenactment of the events of the crucifixion. This latter position can hardly be included among the exemplary features of the Reformation doctrine of the Lord's Supper; it represents, rather, one of the limitations of that doctrine. If, as is frequently the case in contemporary Protestant discussions,[53] the death of Jesus on the cross is understood primarily as an expiatory sacrifice, and the words of institution must be directed to the sacrificial death of Jesus, it will hardly be possible to raise convincing theological objections to an understanding of the presence of Christ in the Lord's Supper, or to an interpretation of the eucharistic sacrifice in terms of his death as an expiation.

That presupposition, however, which the Reformers shared with the Latin tradition in Christology and the doctrine of the Lord's Supper requires modification in the light of the results of contemporary exegesis. Even though the concept of the cross of Christ as a sacrifice is clearly one of the interpretations found in the New Testament, it is not the only explanation of this event, certainly not in the specific manner in which later theology interpreted it as an expiatory sacrifice brought by Jesus as a human being in order to reconcile God. In addition, the fellowship with Jesus which the Eucharist mediates is not to be related to his death in isolation from other aspects of its meaning. Traditional theology sought in a one-sided manner to establish that the Christological basis of the Lord's Supper and of Jesus' gift of salvation was to be found in an understanding of his death on the cross (in an extreme dyotheletic separation of the human and divine in Jesus) as his expiatory sacrifice to the triune God. This needs to be modified by a truly catholic attention to the plurality of motifs which form the Christological background of the Lord's Supper.

Thus many exegetes today stress that the idea of expiation (as expressed in the words of institution that the body of Christ was given "for us," or "for many," and speak of his blood shed "for us") does not necessarily imply the idea of an expiatory sacrifice.[54] The idea of expiation found in the *hyper* formulas is not necessarily identical with the Pauline idea of a new covenant established by the blood of Jesus, or the designation of the blood of Jesus as the blood of the covenant. And serious objections have been advanced against the concept that the words over the cup in the form in which we have them presuppose an understanding of Jesus' death as a covenant sacrifice. Moreover, such a sacrifice is not necessarily an expiatory sacrifice. The basis for these objections is that the shedding of blood simply indicates a violent death and is not part of the terminology of sacrifice.[55] Thus the words over the cup as preserved by Paul simply say that the new covenant is based on the violent death of Jesus. Joachim Jeremias' interpretation of Jesus' last supper as a Passover meal, and the related assumption that Jesus regarded himself as the Passover lamb of the new covenant, has been vigorously disputed. In one passage, Paul calls Jesus "our paschal lamb" (I Cor. 5:7), but he does not make any reference there to the Last Supper, and in his chapter on the Last Supper in the same letter no such connection is drawn. Moreover, Jeremias did not succeed in showing that the blood of the Passover sacrifice had expiatory power. Thus it is not possible by this line of thought to establish that the original meaning of the words over the cup involved an expiatory sacrifice. Scholars such as Hans Lietzmann and Rudolf Bultmann rejected the expiation formula as secondary, because it was apparently not firmly connected with either the words over the bread or those over the cup. In Mark they are connected only with the cup (14:24) and in Paul, only with the bread (I Cor. 11:24), and it is hardly possible to conceive of an omission of the formula from a part of the tradition with which it had been closely connected from the beginning.

In the light of these exegetical conclusions there is no justification for understanding the institution of the Lord's Supper primarily in terms of Jesus' expiatory sacrifice or the presence of Jesus primarily in terms of the crucifixion understood as an expiatory sacrifice. The doctrine of the Lord's Supper is on much firmer ground when it depicts the historical Jesus in whom we participate through the Supper, first of all as the messenger of the coming Kingdom of God, who assures us of future participation in the salvation of the Kingdom through the fellowship which we have with him through the Supper, and thus also assures us of the forgiveness of sins. As a result, the Kingdom itself is already present in the celebration of the Supper as a sign. This starting point does not involve any sacrificial themes.

But fellowship with Jesus is also to be understood as fellowship with the One who was crucified and thus as participation in the meaning of his death on the cross. Insofar as the meaning of Jesus' death for the early church is accurately explained as his dying for us, using the metaphor of sacrifice, there is no reason for denying that our fellowship with Jesus through the Lord's Supper includes participation in his death and in the meaning of that death. In so doing, we need to include the whole breadth of the New Testament witnesses to the meaning of Jesus' death, combining motifs such as the idea of sacrifice and the idea that God was the one who offered up Jesus. This excludes any one-sided "dyotheletic" concept of the death of Jesus as an offering in which God was merely the recipient. Above all, participation of our contemporary celebrations of the Lord's Supper in the meaning of Jesus' death as a sacrifice must be seen in the context of our fellowship with Jesus and his life as vouchsafed to us through the Lord's Supper, and not in isolation as the determining motif in our understanding of the Eucharist. It is hard not to suspect that the concept of sacrifice could in such one-sided a manner come to occupy the foreground in the Christian tradition, not least of all because the liturgist early learned to understand his role as all too similar to that of the priest of the old covenant. If we can overcome the narrowing of the understanding of the Lord's Supper which took place here, then the theological antagonism which has been so deeply entrenched in this theme will be a thing of the past.

VII

In the foregoing discussion it has been assumed that participation in the Lord's Supper brings us into union with the historical Jesus himself. This union and fellowship are inadequately described as "bodily," since they unite with Jesus those who participate in the Supper, far beyond the destruction of those persons' own mortal bodies, so that they may have through him a share in that new life which has already made its appearance in him. But how are we to understand as a reality such fellowship with a historical person belonging to an age that is long past? This raises the question of how we are to think of the presence of Christ in the Lord's Supper.

This question is often ignored in discussions of the doctrine of the Lord's Supper in Protestant and especially Lutheran theology of the present day. It is easy to restrict oneself to Christ's promise contained in the words of institution and to regard the question of the "how" of his presence in the Eucharist as more or less superfluous.[56] Such a conclusion can be regarded as satisfactory only if we accept a formal belief in the authority of the biblical "word" in general and of the words of institution in particular. The questionable nature of such a belief in authority is widely recognized today. If we regard such a position as uncertain ground on which to stand, we will be unable to avoid the question of how that which the words of institution state as a promise can become a reality for us, how it can be related to an understanding of reality which is at all accessible to us. The older theories of the real presence sought to answer this question within the restrictions of the experience of reality current in their own time. This is as true of Luther's doctrines of consubstantiality and ubiquity as it is of the doctrine of transubstantiation of the period of high scholasticism. Thus such theories were by no means dealing with superfluous and clever speculations that did damage to the mystery; they involved unavoidable reflection on the meaning of the reality of the promised presence of Christ. This does not say that such reflection could exhaust the meaning of the promise given in the words of institution by the Lord who invites us to the Supper, whether those words come from the Lord himself or from the interpretation given by the apostolic community. The promise of the real presence of Jesus Christ himself takes precedence over all theories about what it means. This does not make theoretical reflection superfluous, but, with Edward Schillebeeckx, we must recognize it as indispensable if that which is promised is to be understood as reality.[57]

Today it is not possible to say that any of the traditional theories of the real presence give a satisfactory formulation of the eucharistic mystery. This involves more than just the adaptation of traditional formulas to the altered conditions of contemporary thought. It involves the recognition that the contrasting formulations of the presence of Christ in the Lord's Supper which have come to us from the age of the Western denominational divisions were already one-sided and problematic in that age, and for that reason they became the occasion for strife. This is certainly true for the idea of transubstantiation. Neither the ecumenical problems nor the strictly dogmatic problems caused by this theory can be recognized if we regard it as an explanation of the presence of Christ in the Lord's supper which was absolutely valid for a bygone age that was comfortably at home with the categories of Aristotelian philosophy, so that only in the changed situation of the modern age did a new formulation become necessary.[58] The idea of transubstantiation could be seen even in Aristotelian terms as illogical and could therefore be replaced by a symbolic interpretation, or, as with Luther, by a doctrine of ubiquity and consubstantiation, if one were not prepared to accept as a miracle the illogicality of a change of substance without a change of the accidents.

Only in the most recent development of the Catholic doctrine of the Eucharist is there a development through which the doctrine of transubstantiation might lose this appearance of being illogical, that is, by its being involved with the phenomenon of "transignification." This thought was first advanced by the Reformed theologian F. Leenhardt, and then, especially in Catholic circles, was developed through reflection on the context of meaning in which humans perceive reality and in response to changes in that context. The natural occurrences which we are constantly dealing with receive new meaning in the various contexts of human activity. A letter is not only a piece of paper but also the bearer of a message in process of interpersonal communication. The being of things is not something that can be separated from their contexts of meaning, but the meaning that is proper to a thing or an event, or that is given to it, says what the thing or the event really is. The result of this is that the concept of substance must be reinterpreted in terms of the concept of meaning, for substance is nothing other than *to ti ēn einai*—i.e., that which something is by virtue of being that something. If essence or substance is connected with meaning, then substance is no longer, as it was for Aristotle, that basic something unaltered by all change, but it is itself caught up in a process, because that which events and things ultimately mean has not yet been finally determined. Every event and every object is of itself still open to entering into new contexts of meaning, out of which its own meaning will be determined anew. Transubstantiation is therefore no longer a bit of nonsense, but a normal element of structure in the process of the development of the human experience of reality. Such a change of meaning now also takes place when the food of the meal to which Jesus invites us becomes the sign and means for fellowship with him and thereby also with the future of God. This transformation in their meaning cannot be superseded by other experiences of meaning which could modify this bread and this wine, but the change has permanent, eschatological meaning—finality—and therefore determines the final essence of that bread and wine which serve as food in the fellowship at table to which Jesus invites us.[59] Such an interpretation of transubstantiation as transignification and vice versa may be the best theory of the real presence that we can attain today.[60] It advances our understanding of Christ's presence in the Eucharist in a perhaps decisive manner beyond the old difficulties involved in the concept of transubstantiation, in the doctrines of consubstantiation, and in the symbolic interpretation of the Lord's Supper, and at the same time it preserves in itself the elements of truth of all these interpretations.

The symbolic interpretation of the Lord's Supper was correct in that it sought to understand the Supper and its elements as signs of fellowship with Jesus Christ. It was wrong in that it held that the nature of the Supper as a sign was incompatible with the real presence and the essence of that for which the sign stands. Apart from the inadequate formulations of the alternative positions in the theology of that day, this probably was due to a failure to distinguish between symbol and sign. But not every sign is also a symbol. This becomes especially clear where the same thing can be a sign and also in another aspect a symbol. Thus the elements of the Lord's Supper are not only signs of fellowship with Jesus Christ in the meal but they also—although certainly secondarily—are to be interpreted as symbols, that is, symbols of the separation of body and blood in the violent death of Jesus. This symbol is as such to be distinguished from that which it represents, while the designation of bread and wine as body and blood of Christ not only represents something but also gives to the food and drink the meaning that through them Christ himself is united with us. This meaning of bread and wine as signs is fundamental for that which occurs in the Lord's Supper, and it is not to be confused with symbolic interpretations that could attach themselves to it. If this is kept in mind, it is no longer necessary to deny the real presence of Christ in the meal because of the nature of bread and wine as signs, for the real presence is that to which the sacramental signs point.

The Lutheran consubstantiation theory was right in that bread and wine do not through their consecration simply cease to be what they formerly were, but are caught up into participation in the being of Christ, who is present. This being caught up could not be expressed, in view of the state of the discussion of that time, in terms of transubstantiation, in the way that it is today possible for it to be expressed in terms of transignification. In spite of this we must conclude in the light of the situation today that Luther was wrong in his outright rejection of the concept of transubstantiation as mere nonsense. Instead, he could have altered the concept of substance itself, as the current theory of transignification does. But such a demand involves an anachronistic ignoring of the limits that each age imposes on human thought.[61]

The needed change in the Aristotelian concept of substance was not accomplished among those who formulated the eucharistic presence of Christ as transubstantiation. Thus the opposition to the formulation of the dogma in the time of the Reformation cannot simply be regarded as incorrect, although, in the light of our present understanding, that formulation appears relevant if we overlook its inadequate explication by scholastic theology. In addition, the expression "transubstantiation," in the meaning derived from a Christian Aristotelianism, described the event of the Lord's Supper only in terms of a natural occurrence. The idea of transubstantiation, as it was then conceived, did not take into account the constitutive significance of the personal aspects of the Lord's Supper—for example, Jesus' promise that is included, explicitly or implicitly, in the invitation, and on the other hand its being accepted in faith. But the interpretation of transubstantiation as transignification of the elements is the result of Jesus' invitation and is ratified by faith in him as the One to whom God has given all authority, faith that responds to Jesus' invitation. Thus for the first time the decisive points of reference of the Lutheran understanding of the Lord's Supper find through transignification room for expression in the idea of transubstantiation.

This expansion of the concept must bring with it a new understanding of the way that such transubstantiation is accomplished by transignification. Does it lie within the power of the liturgist to accomplish this? The liturgist merely transmits the invitation of Christ. This is seen clearly in that the words of institution are the words of Christ, even though the words transmitted as what Christ himself said may in fact contain elements that were first explicitly formulated in the interpretation given by the church. The transignification is therefore the result of the words of Jesus, and specifically of the historical Jesus. He it is who issues the invitation to fellowship with him at supper. But for the post-Easter church the historical Jesus is not only an object of remembrance but also, as proclaimed in the Easter message, the exalted Lord. The invitation of the historical Jesus derives its present importance from this fact. Because the one who invites is now the exalted Lord, we are to trust him that what he promises will take place, that is, that fellowship with him guarantees participation in the Kingdom of God, in the glory which is already reality for him in his exaltation. In this the identity of the historical Jesus who issues the invitation and the exalted Lord is fundamental for the continuing efficacy of Jesus' invitation and for the present celebration of the Lord's Supper. It is fundamental also for the finality of the transignification of the elements in the issuing of the invitation to the Supper, and thus for its definitive meaning and for making manifest the "substance" of the Supper and of the bread and cup. Nevertheless, the fellowship which the Supper brings is, above all, fellowship with the historical Jesus, with his mission and his cross; it is anamnesis, and only thus is it in a still hidden manner participation in the glory of the One who has been exalted to imperishable life at the right hand of God.

VIII

In view of the meaning which the word that brings about transignification has for the presence of Christ in the celebration of the Lord's Supper, there arises the further question of what is distinctive (*proprium*) in the Supper in contrast to the proclamation of the word. Do not confession of Jesus and faith in him on the basis of the proclamation of Christ bring the same fellowship with him, fellowship that leads us beyond sin and death to participation in the very life of God?

The Lutheran theology of the nineteenth century devoted much attention to the *proprium* of the Lord's Supper.[62] The Eucharist seemed to be devalued if by participating in it the Christian receives no other gift than that which was received through faith in the word that was proclaimed. Gottfried Thomasius saw the distinctive nature of the Lord's Supper in that it mediated Christ's glorified human nature for the nourishment of the inner man, which had been renewed through baptism. This view has been shared by August Vilmar, Rocholl, and others, and is reflected in the present by Sommerlath in his criticism of the Arnoldshain Theses, but it has been vigorously opposed by F. A. Philippi and Hermann Schultz as unbiblical. The interpretation developed by Theodosius Harnack and A. von Oettingen is widely accepted today. It holds that every means of grace bestows one and the same grace, and that there is no difference in the gift of salvation itself but only in the mode of its bestowal. In the present century this solution has been opposed energetically by Paul Althaus.[63] It involves a tendency to stress that the body and blood of Christ cannot be separated from the unity of his living person. This

interpretation is found also in the Arnoldshain Theses, specifically in the second thesis, although it does not state what
constitutes the distinctive nature of the Lord's Supper as a
means of grace in contrast to the other "ways" in which Christ
brings to us the gifts of the good news of salvation. In
theological discussion, insofar as the distinctive nature of the
Lord's Supper is not seen as being in the gift of salvation itself
but in the way in which it is imparted, three features of the
Lord's Supper as a means of grace have been proposed:

1. The personal application of the saving gift in distinction
to the general nature of public proclamation (Philippi and later
writers).

2. The receiving of the elements in the mouth (*manducatio
oralis*), and the distinctively sensory, bodily appropriation of
the saving gift, which is identical with the person of Christ
(Von Oettingen).

3. Involving both the above views, the consolation for the
one who is in doubt concerning his salvation, assuring him that
the Lord's Supper is his personal participation in Christ, with
the undeniable certainty that comes through his bodily experience in that participation (Von Oettingen).

These points of view concerning the nature of the Lord's
Supper have the advantage of resting on the observation of
specific features of the concrete observance of the Eucharist.
At the same time, the phenomenological nature of the distinctive features as means of grace requires broader and deeper
consideration. It is concentrated in too narrow and one-sided a
manner on the interest in the individual's assurance of salvation. This fact and the related Lutheran motif of consolation to
those hard beset, which generally stands in the foreground
when Lutheran theologians consider the question of the distinctive nature of the Lord's Supper, remain central motifs of
devotional life in relation to the Supper. But the subjective
assurance of salvation must be combined with emphasis on the
meaning of the Eucharist for the church, bringing the fellowship of the church into prominence as based on the fellowship
which believers have with Christ. In the shared receiving of
the Eucharist and in the shared liturgical anamnesis of its
institution, the basis of the church's existence becomes clearly

visible. In this connection the *manducatio oralis* has, in its significance for assuring the individual of his salvation, an ecclesiastical dimension as well. Receiving in the mouth the bread and wine which the liturgist has blessed with the words of Christ means that the individual partakes of salvation through an act, which as a bodily act transcends the still unresolved problems raised by the proclamation, and by this act the individual becomes involved in the mysterious depths of the reality of Christ, which the individual will never be able fully to understand.

This subjective side of the oral reception of salvation in the Lord's Supper has been largely overlooked in the past, but it has a direct relevance for the church. Individual believers, as well as the community of those who in faith receive the Lord's Supper, share in the reality of a salvation that unites them far beyond anything they can at present understand—that unites them with Christ and thus also with one another. However necessary it is to begin to understand, so that participation in the Lord's Supper can be experienced for what it is, we are still confronted with the provisional nature of our understanding of the faith in contrast to the profound meaning of the reality of salvation into which the individual enters and in which he has fellowship with others. Thus the reality of fellowship in the church always precedes theological understanding. This can be a liberating insight for a Christianity whose history includes on every hand doctrinal disputes over the meaning of the Eucharist for the church, disputes that have often been overemphasized, because theology itself has lacked the holiness of that reflection which leads to a precise consciousness of the provisional nature of theological formulas. It can also liberate our minds for a new perception of the meaning of the eucharistic celebration. Something of this sort may be active in the movement toward intercommunion, which is growing today in so many Christian communities. Denominational disagreements over the doctrine of the Lord's Supper, like those over the doctrine of church offices and other questions of our Christian understanding of salvation, are often felt to be mere disagreements over our understanding of doctrine and over the ways in which we understand. This entire area has today become problematic in many respects. The Lord's Supper can be explained as the expression of a fellowship which transcends the provisional nature of all human understanding, fellowship with Jesus Christ and also with the church, and which brings into being an ecclesiastical reality of an entirely new sort, an ecumenical catholicity. It is impossible simply to leap over the historically established denominational differences among the major churches, without divorcing the Christian faith from culture in its linguistic and institutional expressions. Therefore it is necessary to take a deep breath and be patient in the tiring process of increased mutual contacts, recognition, and relationships. But if this is possible in any area, then it is possible in the Lord's Supper, where the one Lord of the one church is present and binds the participants together as his community, in order that they may experience the goal of this process of the unification of Christians as being already present and active, so that the process in which the churches grow closer to each other will not stagnate.

10
The Unity of the Church
and the Unity of Mankind

I

The Commission on Faith and Order of the World Council of Churches at its meeting in Bristol, England, in 1967 considered the question of what function the church has "in the light of God's plan for uniting the world. What relationship is there between the search for the unity of the churches with one another and the hope for the unity of mankind?" A year later the full assembly of the World Council in Uppsala provided the impetus to a more thorough study of this theme. The first results appeared in 1970 in the study document "Unity of the Church—Unity of Mankind."[64] In 1971 this was the central theme of the Faith and Order conference in Löwen.[65]

The development of this discussion, which involved also the self-understanding of the ecumenical movement, led beyond the concerns of the church with its own interests to the question of how to combine the search for Christian unity with the church's contribution toward uniting mankind.[66] The questions in social ethics which the Church and Society Movement has raised and the efforts it has exerted were thus to be included in the church's theological self-understanding.

Soon, however, concern was expressed that by taking such a secular orientation in anthropology and social ethics the ecumenical movement might be missing the real nature of the church, and that far from being necessary to the unity of the church this orientation was hindering it.[67] Many Christians came to feel a "great sorrow . . . that their church was losing the substance of its faith because of the progress of ecumenical involvement."[68]

Such concerns must be taken seriously. There is a theologically superficial enthusiasm that makes involvement in social ethics a substitute for the substance of an uncertain faith. Such a position creates mistrust and hampers and delays progress toward Christian unity. Moreover, the impetus will be lacking which the unity of the Christian churches could provide for human community in the midst of all its conflicts and divisions. The most important contribution that Christians can make to human unity would certainly be to regain their own unity. The path to this goal lies through mutual recognition of one another in faith, and this must find its expression in the achievement of sacramental fellowship.

To be sure, the church is not an end in itself. It already manifests the future fellowship of the Kingdom of God, which is to include all mankind, a renewed mankind that has passed through the judgment of God. For the community of mankind can be realized only through overcoming the evil in its midst by means of God's judgment on that evil. The church is already called even now, as the 1968 Assembly of the World Council in Uppsala said, to be the "sign of the future unity of mankind." This statement is in essential agreement with the statement made five years earlier by the Second Vatican Council in the introduction to the Dogmatic Constitution on the Church, where it says, "The Church is a kind of sacrament or sign of intimate union with God, and of the unity of all mankind." The church's role as sacrament, that is as an effective sign of the common future of mankind in the Kingdom of God, points far beyond the false alternatives which were posed in the discussions following Uppsala: whether the future unity of mankind is promised as something that God will bring about and humans have merely to accept, or whether it is the task of the church to bring about this unity. Human effort cannot bring it about, but to work toward it is a natural consequence of the sacramental nature of the church as an effective sign of this future destiny of mankind. A part of its nature as a sign is that the church cannot be understood as a goal in itself, but has as its goal the future Kingdom of God over all mankind.[69] The content of that hope for God's Kingdom is the unity of mankind, that is, human fellowship in peace and justice. As an effective sign of this hope, the church therefore, if it is true to its God-given origin and essence, is to promote peace and justice throughout the world.

The church can be an effective sign of the future unity of humanity only if the church itself is one. In our present situation in which the churches are divided and in view of the painful slowness of ecumenical agreement among the separated churches, so disappointing to the expectations of the world, the church is not fulfilling today for mankind, at least not yet, the function of such a sign. Instead, its own fragmentation reflects the divided state of the world. Thus the unity of the church is not merely a desirable goal for Christians, but one without whose realization the church cannot still exist. It appears that the churches lead a comfortable existence as they are presently constituted and are in no particular hurry to achieve unity. But they must be reminded that without the unity of Christians, no church is a church in the full sense of the word. None of the present separated churches is today identical with the one church of Christ. Are the Orthodox churches and the Roman Catholic Church correct in regarding the Protestant churches as defective, incomplete realizations of the essence of the church? If, however, they regard Protestant Christians as Christians at all and acknowledge that there is anything of the church in their communities, in however defective a form, do they not have to admit that their own church is also defective as long as it has not achieved the visible unity of all Christians?

If without the unity of all Christians the church in the fullest sense has not yet been realized, then the issue in the ecumenical discussions and activities is to work toward the complete form of that church of which both the Second Vatican Council and the World Council Assembly in Uppsala spoke. This church which is an object of faith can, however, take form and become visible in our contemporary Christianity only in the multiplicity of the existing Christian communities, only through mutual recognition of these different communities, which will then develop new forms for the expression of their unity.

It is not possible to attain Christian unity today by ending the multiplicity of Christian churches and theological traditions in order to achieve a new uniformity in doctrine and organization. That such uniformity is not attainable does not constitute a flaw in the ecumenical situation. On the contrary, it provides a real opportunity for an ecumenical understanding throughout Christianity. If the whole of the Christian world were to become today a unified church with strictly unified doctrine, a uniform hierarchical organization, and a uniform liturgy, it would be a source of trauma for all non-Christian religions and world views. It would be just as exclusive toward the outside world as it would be uniform within, and that means that such a church could no more be a sign for the unity of mankind than could the church of the Middle Ages. The repressive features that accompany uniformity would produce a new distortion of the church's image. On the other hand, a unity of Christians through reciprocal recognition in faith and love, accompanied by continuing differences in doctrine and polity because of the shared knowledge that one's own faith and polity are provisional—this kind of Christian unity would have no need to shut itself off from other religions in an exclusivistic attitude. If a Christian knows how provisional his or her own insights and way of life are, then that Christian will be able to bring to the encounter with persons who live on the basis of non-Christian traditions an awareness that their lives may be related to the same divine mystery to which his own Christian faith is related. This by no means should detract from the passion that a believer has for the truths of his own religion. If we Christians have received in Jesus Christ the final "eschatological" criterion for determining how far or near each person is to God's future, this still does not mean that all persons whom Christ will one day acknowledge as his own must become Christians. Even among those who do not confess themselves to be followers of Christ, the faith and love of Christians will discover signs that there are those who belong to God's future, which Jesus proclaimed, and therefore also belong to Jesus. But even where this is not the case, the

Christian should be fully aware that according to the message of the New Testament it is not we but the Christ who is coming again who will decide whose life and conduct are faithful to the norm of the Kingdom of God which he proclaimed.

The knowledge that a person can belong to Christ and to the Kingdom which Christ proclaimed, even though for one reason or another the person did not confess Christ, while many "Christians" will not enter into the coming Kingdom of God because their actual lives did not correspond to the message of Jesus—this knowledge should from the beginning of Christian history have had the effect of eliminating all Christian intolerance. In any case, it makes it possible for us today to have a less inhibited relationship with those who live in other religious traditions. It makes it possible to recognize freely that in these other traditions as well there is concern for the future unity of humanity, and that the other religions can make a contribution toward that unity. Christians and non-Christians alike can share the insight that if they are to achieve their human destiny of unity through peace and justice, they must achieve it through unity with God. This basic insight into the meaning of religion for the unity of mankind can grow in spite of remaining disagreements in our understanding of God and of the ways in which God is to be worshiped. It can also be the starting point for a new closeness even in areas of disagreement. This closeness has already been partially achieved as the result of reciprocal relationships between the Christian and non-Christian religious traditions.

In all this we must not overlook the difference between the movement toward the ecumenical unity of Christianity and the efforts toward ecumenical understanding with non-Christian religions. The dialogue within Christianity is concerned with giving form to the unity of the Christian faith beyond all differences in our understanding of the faith and of church organization. The dialogue with other religions, at least under present circumstances, does not lead in the same way to a unity of confession under the criterion of a common faith. Yet even here, and certainly in differing degree in relationships with the various religions, we can also discover things that we have in common, the knowledge of which can basically alter the future relationship between Christians and non-Christians. Only in the framework of such a development, which would overcome the religious hatred of the past without sacrificing our Christian identity, can a reunited Christian church become the sign and instrument of the unity of mankind. In all this the old Christian virtue of humility, of knowing the distance between our own knowledge and way of life and the fullness of the mystery of God's future, holds the key, both to a new experience of unity in faith among Christians and to greater understanding with those who come from non-Christian religious traditions.

II

Is the "ecumenical utopia" an illusion? Are the unity of the church and the unity of mankind ideas that merely arouse an enthusiastic idealism that is out of touch with reality and that therefore can perpetuate, undisturbed, many forms of social and ecclesiastical reality that differ sharply from those ideals?

The real human situation is characterized by competition and conflicting interests, by the arrogance of conquerors and rulers, by the resentment of the disadvantaged, by violent liberation and new oppression. Humanity is fragmented by conflicts between tribes, peoples, and races. In some parts of the world today nationalism may be essential as a unifying power to overcome the particularity of tribal rivalries and entrenched caste interests. But from the sad experiences of Europe the lesson should be drawn that the result will be even deeper divisions between nations. There is no straight road that leads from nationalism to the unification of mankind, except for the old road that always ends in collapse, the road of the formation of imperial power, its extension, and its defense through oppression, colonialism, and war.

Such conflicts not only separate peoples from one another, but within peoples and nations they set the rulers and the ruled against each other. In the socialist countries the situation is not different from that in the traditional monarchies or in the democracies of the West, even though in the democracies the situation is improved through provisions for the control of power and for the peaceful change of government. In order to preserve the unity of society against the centrifugal tendencies of private interests of individuals and groups, there is a universal need for force, the silent force of relationships and the pressure for conformity, and where that does not succeed, the brutal force of the power of the state.

In spite of all this, there is in today's world a growing movement toward unity. The modern development of the economy and of transportation and communication has produced an increased tightening of the bonds that unite regions that are widely separated geographically. It has increased the mutual dependence of peoples and nations to a degree previously unknown. The development of the techniques of war has produced a movement toward peace, at least among the largest and technologically most advanced powers, because the full commitment of the weapons of destruction would lead to self-destruction. This situation, however, remains fluid enough and does not exclude the possibility of "limited conflicts," which for the nations involved are no less gruesome, and often more gruesome than most earlier wars.

This increase of mutual dependence among peoples and nations does not yet mean a higher degree of community, of peace in the deeper sense of friendship among the nations, or of justice in universally accepted relationships free of violence in our life together. The increasing density of population and the growing complexity of the net of technical and organizational interdependence serves rather to increase aggression or to cause people to withdraw into private areas of freedom and thus of indifference toward one another. But the overemphasis on the private sphere creates a feeling of meaninglessness, and the contrast between a person's assumed freedom from social responsibility and the actual harm done to others through the use of such freedom compels society to restrict it. Only the development of a sense of community of mutual respect and concern can lead us beyond such dilemmas. The increase of interdependence in our human life together brings with it increasing pressures, and the more unbearable these pressures become, the more necessary it is to find solutions in the sense of the formation of a community that can deal with these problems. Only in this sense does this growing interdependence provide opportunities for a growing unity or community of mankind.

In taking the difficult step from the pressure of increasing interdependence to a solution through new forms of human community, we should expect help or at least inspiration from the religions. Many religious traditions have developed a consciousness that human beings belong together and therefore they have established for us models of social virtues. At the same time, the religions have compromised themselves in many ways, in that their connection with the ruling authorities and their legitimizing of existing conditions have led them to fail to articulate the impulses toward humanizing the conditions of life, or to leave those impulses weak. Religious fanaticism has had even worse effects, as the divisiveness and the mutual condemnations of the religions have led to persecutions and religious wars, the worst examples of which in the realm of Christianity are the Crusades and the persecutions of the Jews. Even within the major religious communities there have been denominational divisions, the parties to which often fought each other with greater intolerance, as seen especially in the European wars of religion that resulted from the church divisions of the sixteenth century, the inestimable consequences of which can still be felt today.

The conflicts of religious systems could appear tolerable as long as they broke out only on the periphery of religiously homogenous cultures, or (as was the case in Christianity and especially in Protestantism in the nineteenth century) when the goal of Christianizing the world by reducing the other religions to a marginal position was pursued in connection with the colonial expansion of the European powers. Today it is recognized that religious pluralism cannot be eliminated, either in relationship to non-Christian religions or within Christianity itself. Protestantism cannot regard the Roman Catholic and the Orthodox churches as relics of a bygone age doomed to wither away, and Catholicism can no longer await a restoration of Christian unity by a return of Protestants to Rome.

As a result of the spread of European secularism through industrial technology, there is a worldwide situation today like that which developed in Europe as the result of the denominational wars of the sixteenth and seventeenth centuries. In that period the political unity of society in the form of the state could be preserved only by excluding all religious differences, although it was still believed that the political unity of society needed the basis of a unified religion. This led to the development of a civil religion that was distinguished from the Christian denominations but that led in turn to religion becoming a private matter in its disputatious, denominational forms. Perhaps religion could not so easily have been made a private matter if this step could not so readily be justified, at least in Protestantism, in terms of one's religious consciousness, as a result of the religious freedom won by the Reformation. Although religion became a private matter, its public influence was not ended. It continued to make itself felt through the subjective attitudes of individual citizens, insofar as their religious attitudes could still motivate them to place the common good, as they saw it, above particular private interests. Even so, the private nature of religion, in contrast to the unity of the political and economic organization of society, led to a weakening of religious consciousness, because if religious convictions are a private matter, they inevitably are seen as arbitrary and nonbinding. This situation was especially favorable to the growth of conservative expressions of the religious traditions, which kept their understanding of truth separate from their reflections on the social factors involved in their own faith. On the other hand, the conservative forms of belief, especially in their conflicts with one another, reinforced the necessity of religious neutrality on the part of state and society. The liberalization of the religious traditions, however, has failed, especially since its awareness of its own subjectivity prevents it from establishing a positive relationship with the scientific understanding of truth. Both of these developments have contributed to the present impotence of the religious consciousness in the face of the task of bringing about human unity and of mastering the problems of increasing interdependence by providing new forms of society, and doing so in a way that corresponds to the best impulses of both the Christian faith and other traditions. We have a right, however, to expect the religions to perform these tasks.

III

The basic issue to be confronted in the search for a possible contribution of religion to the unification of mankind is the clarification of the question raised by the sociology of religion: What is the function of religion in achieving the unity of society? The unity of mankind can be achieved only by an alteration in the relationship of nations to one another, and this is dependent on the inner development of their social systems. If religious convictions were by nature merely a private matter, they could have no influence at all on this process, at least not on its appropriate development. But religion is not a private matter, because religious talk about God must claim to be valid for interpersonal relationships. God would not be God, in the sense of the reality that determines everything, if he were only the God of the one who professes faith in him. The claim of religion to interpersonal validity brings to light the peculiar and problematic nature of the position that religion is a private matter, as it developed in the modern political world.

Since Émile Durkheim, the modern sociology of religion has recognized the social function of religion in establishing the themes of the value system that is the basis of social life as a whole and of the context of meaning within which social life unfolds. At the same time, it is a social subsystem of that society.[70] In medieval society—that is, at a comparatively high stage of the differentiation of the various subsystems of society[71]—it was the Christian religion that determined the self-understanding of society as a whole in relation to its subsystems. To be sure, basing the unity of society on the unity of faith brought with it in the Byzantine Empire and in the Christian Middle Ages that dogmatic intolerance which proved to be the decisive weakness of the medieval system and which brought about its downfall. This shortcoming, however, does not falsify the fundamental assumption that the unity of society and its political order needs a religious basis.[72] It is certainly not one of the accomplishments of modern middle-class society, but rather one of its unsolved problems, that after the end of the religious wars of the sixteenth and seventeenth centuries, society had to define itself as neutral in matters of religion in order to be free from the mutually destructive fury of the degenerate dogmatic intolerance of quarreling religious parties. In the seventeenth century this step was to some degree inescapable if political order was to survive, but the problem it brings with it is that if the above-mentioned assumption proves true, a society cannot remain neutral toward religion. The thesis of the neutrality of a whole society and its political order is a modern example of self-deception. It can be explained in terms of the historical situation in which it arose, which demanded that religious beliefs be a private matter, but since it concerns the actual presuppositions on which the unity of a society's life rests, it is not without its dangers. It is the probable cause of the proliferation of civil religion, especially nationalism, in modern history, and also of the abnormal growth of economic interests in modern capitalism. Similarly, in the socialist countries Marxism has taken over the sociological function of religion as the ideology that provides the basis for the unity of meaning in the life of society.

Religion is indispensable for life in society, because the conflicts between the individual and society in the arena of the economic and political order are unavoidable.[73] If these conflicts could be avoided, if the struggle between the individual and society could be eliminated by political and economic changes, and a truly human society could be established, as Marx thought possible, then religion would be truly unnecessary for society, as he predicted. But it seems to be the case that the conflicts between the individual and society cannot be solved politically or economically, but only in religious terms. If the justification for the political order is based on the difference between the total interests of society and the special interests of individuals and groups, and on the necessity of attaining the general interest in contrast to those special interests, it is still true that the general interest can be given expression and made to prevail only by specific individuals or elite groups operating against other individuals and groups. It is therefore inescapably connected with the private interests of those ruling individuals and elite groups, regardless of whether the state takes the form of a monarchy, an aristocracy, a democracy, or a socialist state. As long as the general interest of the society, the common good, must be maintained by certain individuals in opposition to the rest of society, authority is being exercised, and conflicts arise between the rulers and the ruled, however the political system may be constructed. Such authority can be tolerated only on condition that the individuals who rule do so in loyalty to a "truth" that is superior to them and to all other members of the society and not subject to their whims. At least they must promote and maintain the belief that this is the case. The binding power which a "truth" that is accepted as superior has on the rulers cannot be merely based on laws, because they are subject to human legislative processes, and, even where there is a separation of powers, laws are seldom completely removed from the whims of the rulers. Moreover, their formulation requires standards, values, and accepted meanings that guide and direct the legislative process.

Neither can the "truth" to which the ruling authority appeals for its legitimation be scientific truth in the sense of the physical sciences, because they do not encompass the total meaning of a society's life. That is the function of religion, and it is on this basis that authority must legitimize itself and assure itself of the loyalty of those who are ruled. Authority needs the truths of a religious faith to which it is subject in order to establish its legitimacy. Even the secular states of the modern age could not escape this necessity. As a consequence of relegating the denominational expressions of Christianity to the realm of private belief, the state has sought the basis for its legitimacy in "natural religion," as even today most constitutions make clear, or in conceptions which, because of the principle of the religious neutrality of the state, do not appear to be either religious or substitutes for religion, though that is what they really are. These include such varied forms of civil religion as the idea of the sovereignty of the people, nationalism, and a variety of world views. The trouble with all these synthetic formulations is that their contents lack true transcendence, and therefore they are by nature, and not through abuse, ideological. The "people" is never sovereign, for everywhere authority really is in the hands of an elite minority. The nation exists only in the totality of the individuals, whom the ruling elite integrate into a unit. World views would be superior to the will of the rulers only if they really were "scientific" in nature, and their alleged scientific character were not based on the assertions of the ruling class, but represented a commitment to a truth that they accepted as superior. Because it is usually the case that those who hold authority really believe that the will of the people, the nation, and the current world view represent normative instances of universal validity that are givens, those concepts take on actual religious functions and are surrounded by a religious aura. Thus the modern relegation of religious positions to the private sphere has not resulted in the religious neutrality of the state. Instead, under this pretense other standards have taken over the function of religion as constitutive of the meaning of life in society, enabling the state to regulate its relation to traditional religion, now denominationalized and private, in a different manner. Setting up the sovereignty of the people as the basis of natural religion is much closer to certain elements that the Christian denominations hold in common, in spite of their disagreements, than it is to nationalism or the world views of fascism or Marxism. It has become evident that the idea of the sovereignty of the people must be supplemented, either by a theocratic Calvinism (as was the case in its beginnings) or by nationalism, or liberalism, or some other political world view, in order to establish norms by which a society can understand its own meaning.

It is characteristic of the political history of the modern age that the fact of authority as such has become the central feature of social criticism. Because religion has been reduced to a private matter, it is no longer possible to give religious justification to authority on the basis of its relation to a truth that is superior to it. But in addition, the various forms of political substitutes for religion could not appear believable for long, because they lack transcendence, are not independent of the will of the ruler, and do not derive their authority from a

norm that is binding on those in power as well as on all other
members of the society. As a result, the great majority of
individuals see power as naked repression, exercised by some
of their number who through chance, circumstances, or in-
trigue, but without any deeper right, have come into power.
But such power is intolerable. Therefore the rulers must keep
it a secret that authority in the sense of responsibility for the
tasks of the whole society will inevitably be exercised by a few
individuals. They maintain this secret by ideologies which
assert that relationships of authority are not permanent, but in
this way they call forth criticism that unmasks what they are
doing. When the critics discover the camouflage in such
ideologies, they stir up moral indignation that threatens the
status quo, because they harbor the further illusion that the
authority which some exercise over others can be overthrown.
But what can be achieved is to establish norms to which
authority is subject. It is this which is the function of religion in
social systems. The task is to overcome the dilemma of the
modern problem of authority: the sharp alternative between
blinding oneself and others through ideology and the revolt of
those who strip ideologies bare but are themselves also blind-
ed. This will require a redefining and renewal of the role of
religion in society in a way that will do justice to its fundamental function without falling back into the dogmatism and
intolerance of denominations that fought each other to the
death. It was by overcoming that dogmatism that the modern
political world arose.

IV

The ecumenical movement of the present century has
opened the way within Christianity for an understanding of the
possibility of church unity without doctrinal uniformity. Unity
in the faith seems possible without doctrinal consensus in the
traditional sense. Of course the position that unity in faith and
disagreements in our understanding of the faith are not mutually exclusive is itself a doctrinal statement. But neither this nor
any other doctrinal statement is to be regarded as identical
with the final form of the truth of the faith. This is prevented by

the decisive insight that all theological formulations are provisional. This insight—which is motivated by the eschatological awareness in the Christian tradition and by the awareness of the distance that separates the present-day Christian, the *homo viator,* from the final consummation—constitutes the basis for the possibility of recognizing other forms of understanding the faith as valid expressions of concern for the same truth which one's own formulation is intended to express. Of course such recognition both precedes and requires efforts on both sides toward a common formulation of the common faith. We must remember that the struggle to attain it will not reach a decisive conclusion before the end of time and history, and that every agreement that is reached will be only an intermediate stage.

Today it no longer seems impossible to bring about the unity of the separated churches by a mutual recognition of the unity of the faith even in the midst of a continuing multiplicity of differing and always limited perspectives in our understanding of the faith and of the forms of church life. It should not be an insuperable difficulty for any Christian denomination to interpret its own tradition in this sense without being untrue to its substance. By expanding our view beyond the narrow confines of our own formulations of the faith, we can claim the full breadth of catholicity in a new way for our own tradition. The mutual recognition of one another in the faith, the acceptance of full fellowship in the church, will then make it possible to develop new institutional expressions of Christian unity amidst the multiplicity of its continuing traditions and separate communities.

Through the ecumenical process by which Christians are drawn closer together, there have come about, for the first time since the division of the Western church in the sixteenth century, the conditions for bringing about a reversal of the situation in which religion is a private matter, a situation which constituted the starting point for modern political development and placed apparently insuperable difficulties in the way of any contributions that the religious traditions might make to the future unity of mankind. Such a reversal cannot mean a return to denominational control of society any more than an ecumenical unity of Christianity can mean a return to dogmatic conformity and religious intolerance. The movement toward accepting the multiplicity that exists in the actual situation in the Christian world is increasingly felt in the individual denominations themselves. It is the guarantee that the principle of religious freedom will be the basis of any conceivable Christian union, and also the basis of the self-understanding of every future form of Christianity as a whole. This also alters the relationship of Christianity to the non-Christian religious traditions. Even though this aspect of the ecumenical process must take a different form, it is still possible to foresee a situation in which the religions would not have so exclusive an attitude toward one another, but by overcoming their fragmentation, even though around different centers, would be able to articulate more clearly than they can today the conscience of mankind.

The first concern of the ecumenical movement must remain the unity of Christianity, because the church is nowhere fully realized if it is not the one, universal church, which is found in the local and regional churches. But the Christian ecumenical movement cannot accomplish this mission without at the same time creating a model for the compatibility of unity and multiplicity in relation to the other religions and in the political world as well. The ecumenical movement can make a contribution toward the unity of all mankind not only by taking Christian positions on the contemporary problems of secular society but, more importantly and decisively, through overcoming its own basic problems that delay the unity of the church.

Notes

1. This view was formulated by E. Vogelsang, as cited in J. Koopmans, *Das altkirchliche Dogma in der Reformation* (1955), p. 102.

2. Melanchthon expressed this in his new draft of the doctoral oath of the University of Wittenberg (O. Ritschl, *Dogmengeschichte des Protestantismus*, Vol. I [1908], pp. 231ff.), and Calvin expressed it in his appeal to the consensus of the early church (ibid., pp. 354f.).

3. F. Chr. Baur, *Die Epochen der kirchlichen Geschichtsschreibung* (1852), pp. 48f. The quotation that follows is found on p. 50.

4. In the current Catholic doctrine of grace, the term "extrinsicality" denotes an understanding of grace in which there is no inner relationship to the concept of nature. It would appear that this merely gives extreme emphasis to the independence of grace from human nature, but in reality the unintended consequence is that human nature is made independent, unrelated to and contrasted to grace, so that human nature of itself no longer seems to be in need of grace.

5. H. von Campenhausen, "Das Bekenntnis im Urchristentum," *Zeitschrift für die neutestamentliche Wissenschaft* 63 (1972), p. 214.

6. Ibid., pp. 235ff., 241ff.

7. K. Raiser (ed.), *Löwen 1971: Studienberichte und Dokumente der Kommission für Glauben und Kirchenverfassung*, Supplement 18/19 to *Ökumenische Rundschau* (1971), p. 78.

8. H. Fries in *Catholica* 27 (1973), p. 191; *Una Sancta* 25 (1970), pp. 107–115.

9. E.g., G. Gassmann, *Lutherische Monatshefte* (1973), pp. 195ff.; also *KNA* 20 (May 9, 1973). Gassmann rightly points to the fact that in certain preliminary studies—as distinguished from the theses—there are occasions where the differences involved in "unity in multiplicity" could have been described.

10. W. Kasper, "Ökumenischer Konsens über das kirchliche

Amt?" *Stimmen der Zeit* 191 (1973), pp. 219–230, esp. pp. 225ff.

11. K. Rahner, "Von Sinn und Auftrag des kirchlichen Amtes," *FAZ,* Feb. 14, 1973, p. 8.

12. K. Lehmann, "Ämteranerkennung und Ordinationsverständnis," *Catholica* 27 (1973), pp. 248–262, esp. p. 250.

13. *Luther* 44 (1973), pp. 49–65, esp. p. 53.

14. *Una Sancta* 25 (1970), III.

15. *Herderkorrespondenz* 27 (1973), p. 384.

16. Ibid., p. 159.

17. G. Hild, *Materialdienst des konfessionskundlichen Instituts in Bensheim* 24 (1973), p. 34.

18. In this connection see W. Kasper, "Zur Frage der Anerkennung der Ämter in den lutherischen Kirchen," *Theologische Quartalsschrift* 151 (1971), pp. 97–104, esp. pp. 99ff. The Reformers were aware of the issues, especially through their reading of Jerome's writings. In a direct appeal to Jerome, Melanchthon wrote in his tractate on the power and primacy of the pope that there is no distinction between "bishops and presbyters, but all clergy are both bishops and presbyters." (*Die Bekenntnisschriften der evang.-luth. Kirche* [1952], pp. 489f. For Luther's similar view, see most recently P. Manns, "Amt und Eucharistie in der Theologie Martin Luthers," in *Amt und Eucharistie,* ed. by P. Bläser [1973], esp. pp. 163f., n. 176.) The distinction between the two offices became accepted "only through human decision." For Melanchthon that is no reason to dismiss this distinction out of hand. Instead, he quotes Jerome further: "The choice of one alone, who had others under him, took place in order to guard against schism." The distinctive superiority of the office of bishop over that of presbyter came about therefore in order to preserve the unity of the church, and in this aspect it is regarded in a consistently positive manner in the Lutheran confessions. Similarly this verdict applies to all offices of leadership beyond the local level, whether regional or universal in scope, and thus to the papacy as well. The development of these offices, when seen in this light, gave expression to a basic feature of church offices in general—responsibility for the unity of all believers. Thus it is not without good reason that the Lutheran confessions state again and again that "for the sake of love and unity" (Schmalkald Articles, III) the privilege of the bishops to ordain and confirm should be respected; further, that pastors and churches should be obedient to the bishops (Augsburg Confession, Art. 28), and that Protestants "are fully ready to help to preserve the old order of the church and the authority of the bishop, if the bishops do not oppose our teachings and will accept our priests" (*Apology for the Augsburg Confession,* 14). The significance of church offices beyond the local level is based on the nature of each office and should be better known and more highly regarded by Protestants. It is important to recognize that without these offices the

visible form of the church lacks something of that unity which the Christian faith confesses.

19. H. Mühlen, "Das mögliche Zentrum der Amtsfrage," *Catholica* 27 (1973), pp. 329–358, esp. p. 350. On pp. 336ff. he refers to J. Aarts, *Die Lehre Martin Luthers über das Amt der Kirche* (Helsinki, 1972); and H. Lieberg, *Amt und Ordination bei Luther und Melanchthon* (1962). Luther's later emphasis on a specific gift of the Spirit for ordination does not, however, as Mühlen seems to assume, stand in opposition to this public nature of the office.

20. Mühlen, "Das mögliche Zentrum der Amtsfrage," p. 350.

21. Ibid., p. 352.

22. Mühlen admits as much on p. 353: "Naturally it makes a difference whether a person is publicly charged with 'responsibility for the common cause'; whether, that is, he not only speaks in front of the congregation but also expressly speaks in its name." This is the thesis of the Memorandum, and when Mühlen continues, such "public commissioning presupposes a special call," he is in complete agreement with the Memorandum. Why then this polemic? The Memorandum does not contend that this call "consists primarily in organizational abilities." Instead, it speaks of ordination as "a call to office in the church" (Thesis 15).

23. Ibid., p. 343.

24. Ibid., p. 353.

25. L. Scheffczyk, "Die Christuspräsentation als Wesensmoment des Priesteramtes," *Catholica* 27 (1973), pp. 293–311. Scheffczyk (p. 297, n. 18) points out that E. Schlink did "accept this idea" in the preliminary studies for the Memorandum held in Heidelberg. He might also have referred to Thesis 7 of the Memorandum itself, which says that the apostles, "as those commissioned by Jesus Christ," are in contrast to the other members of the church.

26. P. E. Persson disagrees in his *Repräsentatio Christi, Der Amtsbegriff in der neueren röm.-katholischen Theologie* (1966), pp. 176f. He argues that the "concept of a 'representation' of the office of Christ by the officers of the church is possible" only through "the distinction between the divine and human in the saving work of Christ," which makes human cooperation with God possible.

27. WA 7, 66, 3ff. Cf. also T. Steudle, *Communio sanctorum beim frühen Martin Luther* (Dissertation, Mainz, 1966), pp. 67ff., 107ff.

28. In agreement with earlier statements of Catholic authors (cf. Persson, *Repräsentatio Christi*, pp. 116ff.), Mühlen does take it into account ("Das mögliche Zentrum der Amtsfrage," pp. 343ff.) that the term "for others" cannot in the first instance mean the representation of Christ by the office-bearer, since this must first of all be ascribed to the priesthood of all believers.

29. Scheffczyk, "Die Christuspräsentation als Wesensmoment des Priesteramtes," pp. 294f.

30. *Reform und Anerkennung kirchlicher Ämter* (1973), 175.

31. K. Rahner and K. Lehmann, "Kerygma und Dogma," *Mysterium Salutis* I (1965), esp. pp. 693–696.

32. Lehmann, "Ämteranerkennung und Ordinationsverständnis," *Catholica*, 27 (1973), pp. 248–262. Lehmann holds (p. 254) that the theses of the Memorandum do not preserve the nature of ordination, since they pass over the question of the effectiveness of the symbolic actions in reference to the grace that is promised. This may involve a misunderstanding of Thesis 15, which describes ordination as the conferring of the authority that accompanies the call to the office. In this light the understanding of the concept of promise used in the final sentence of Thesis 15 may be interpreted in the sense of effective promise. It would certainly have increased the precision of the formulation if the concept of effective promise had been expressly used here. In addition the thesis could have clarified the concepts "conferring of authority" and "promise" by reference to the meaning of epiclesis in the act of ordination. In any case, the immediately preceding Thesis 14 speaks of a "call of God in the power of the one Spirit of Jesus Christ."

33. *Reform und Anerkennung kirchlicher Ämter* (1973), p. 198.

34. Ibid., p. 193. Mühlen ("Das mögliche Zentrum ·der Amtsfrage," p. 351) is right to question this. He asks. "Why is this dimension not an explicit theme in the 'Theses'?" That this is mentioned in Thesis 16 as one possibility among others can be explained in that the Theses contain only what was accepted by all the Institutes. The explanation is the same for the situation which arouses Mühlen's astonishment, that according to Thesis 17 only "many" regard the commitment of the entire existence of the one who is ordained as being "the religious uniqueness of the office."

35. Lehmann ("Ämteranerkennung und Ordinationsverständnis," p. 250) rightly objected to a lack of clarity in the last sentence of Thesis 15. It says that the participating Institutes could not attain complete agreement on the relationship of ordination and the charisma of office. This involves in particular the question of whether ordination presupposes a charismatic call to office in the church, a call that is to be distinguished from ordination itself, or whether this call takes place through the act of ordination, or how these two points of view are to be combined. Thesis 15 characterizes ordination itself as a call, so that this point of view stands in the foreground, and the concluding sentence emphasizes that such a call is connected with the promise of the charisma of office. In addition, however, it allows for individual cases in which it might be possible to understand ordination as the confirmation of a charisma that has already been received. A limiting of ordination to the recognition of an existing charisma is directly avoided. To this extent the Memorandum, in contrast to the assumption of Lehmann (p. 250), takes into account the comment

made by E. Schlink in the volume *Reform und Anerkennung kirchlicher Ämter* (1973), p. 134, no. 10.

36. Kasper, "Ökumenischer Konsens über das kirchliche Amt?" pp. 219–230.

37. P. Althaus, *Die christliche Wahrheit*, 3d ed (1952), pp. 536ff. W. Trillhaas, in his *Dogmatik* (1962), pp. 354ff., discusses the concept of sacrament in his transition between the sections on baptism and the Lord's Supper.

38. W. Elert, *Der christliche Glaube*, 3d ed. (1956), pp. 355ff. Baptism and the Lord's Supper are incorporated into Elert's work in differing ways. The Lord's Supper is concerned with Christ's work of reconciliation (Ch. 13), while baptism is discussed in connection with the church (Ch. 15). Althaus himself points out that, leaving aside Schleiermacher, who wanted to eliminate the concept of sacrament entirely, G. Thomasius, Luthardt, and A. Schlatter discussed it only following their consideration of baptism and the Lord's Supper.

39. Althaus, *Die christliche Wahrheit*, p. 537.

40. Elert, *Der christliche Glaube*, p. 362. If Christ "did not give" the instruction to repeat the observance, then "the Lord's Supper ceases to be an institution given by Christ."

41. Althaus, *Die christliche Wahrheit*, p. 566. Similarly Trillhaas in his *Dogmatik*, pp. 367f.

42. Althaus, ibid., p. 568.

43. H. Gollwitzer, in *Gespräch über das Abendmahl* (Berlin, 1959), p. 24.

44. P. Brunner, in *Gespräch über das Abendmahl*, p. 53. But when Brunner continues, "On the other hand, the table fellowship of the risen Lord with his disciples in the time of his visible Easter appearances must be included in the occasions of institution," it is necessary to draw a distinction in terms of the foregoing discussion. The Easter experiences could renew and reinforce the prior institution of the eschatological meal, but in so doing they clearly presuppose it.

45. Ibid., p. 54.

46. For Catholic theology see J. Powers, *Eucharistie in neuer Sicht* (1968), pp. 75ff.; also especially works by P. Schoonenberg; also E. Schillebeeckx, *Die eucharistische Gegenwart*, 2d ed. (1968), pp. 68f., 80ff., 93 [cf. E. Schillebeeckx, *The Eucharist* (Sheed Andrews & McMeel, 1968)]. In Lutheran theology since the time of Harnack and Oettingen the personal character of the gift of the Lord's Supper has received increasing emphasis, most recently especially from P. Althaus, in contrast to another direction, which sought to find in the body and blood of Christ, as such, that which is special in the gift of the Eucharist. In the nineteenth century this was represented chiefly by G. Thomasius. On this point, see E. M. Skibbe, "Das Proprium des Abendmahls," *Kerygma und Dogma* 10 (1964), pp. 78–122.

47. Brunner, in *Gespräch über das Abendmahl*, pp. 63f.

48. In this connection, see H. C. Seraphim, *Von der Darbringung des Leibes Christi in der Messe: Studien zur Auslegungsgeschichte des römischen Messkanons und Erwägungen zur Messopferlehre* (Dissertation, Munich, 1970). There the concept of a sacramental presentation of Christ by the priest is portrayed as the result of the process of transformation being concentrated on the recitation of the words of institution. As the result of such concentration it was easy to understand the sacrificial terminology in the following prayers as implying an offering of Christ, who was sacramentally present.

49. This is recognized today by Protestants, for example, A. Buchrucker, "Die Repräsentation des Opfers Christi im Abendmahl in der gegenwärtigen katholischen Theologie," *Kerygma und Dogma* 13 (1967), pp. 273–296, esp. pp. 278ff.

50. See K. H. Bieritz, "Oblatio Ecclesiae," *Theologische Literaturzeitung* 94 (1969), pp. 241–251, esp. pp. 249f. An especially important work is H.-J. Schulz, "Christusverkündigung und kirchlicher Opfervollzug nach den Anamnesetexten der eucharistischen Hochgebete," in *Christuszeugnis der Kirche (Festschrift Bischof Hengsbach)*, ed. by P. W. Scheele and G. Schneider (1970), pp. 93–128.

51. See Buchrucker, "Die Repräsentation des Opfers Christi im Abendmahl," pp. 294f., in reference to R. Prenter, *Kerygma und Dogma* 1 (1955), p. 53.

52. E. Iserloh, *Abendmahl und Opfer* (1960), p. 103. See also the comments of Max Thurian in *Eucharistie* (1963; Festschrift for Pierre du Moulin), pp. 229f.

53. Reference should be made here to the role of the concept of sacrifice in the Bonn and Heidelberg formulas from the period of preliminary studies for the Arnoldshain Theses (quoted by P. Brunner in *Gespräch über das Abendmahl*, p. 59.) What W. Averbeck wrote in *Der Opfercharakter des Abendmahls in der neueren evangelischen Theologie* (1966), esp. p. 787, concerning the Christological background of the denominational disagreements over the nature of the Lord's Supper as sacrifice requires modification. The decisive factor is not the differing estimate ("latreutic" or "soteriological") of the significance of Jesus' humanity in the crucifixion, though this must be noted. It is not this that is decisive for the rejection of the Mass as a sacrifice, but the Protestant reluctance to permit at this point a participation of the believer, or of the church, in Christ's work. Here the Reformation position became involved in internal contradictions, because Luther in particular elsewhere stressed the full participation of the believer in Christ through faith.

54. E. Lohse distinguished between the substitutionary expiatory death of martyrs and righteous persons and sacrifice in a ritual sense (*Märtyrer und Gottesknecht* [1955], p. 126). The concept of covenant,

which he regarded as a Hellenistic supplement, introduced the idea that the death of Jesus was to be understood as a sacrifice which instituted the covenant.

55. E. Lohmeyer, "Vom urchristlichen Abendmahl," *Theologische Rundschau* 9 (1937), p. 189, in connection with his criticism of Jeremias' interpretation of the blood as the blood of Passover. See also H. Patsch, *Abendmahl und historischer Jesus* (1972), pp. 86f.

56. Elert (*Der christliche Glaube*, p. 382) even calls the real presence itself a mere "auxiliary concept." Althaus (*Die christliche Wahrheit*, p. 581) terms it an "offence against the Gospel" that the Roman church "has declared as a dogma of the church a metaphysical theory of the miracle of the real presence, a theory that stands or falls with Aristotelian philosophy." Today most Catholic writers on the dogma of transubstantiation deny that this is the case. Cf. Schillebeeckx, *Die eucharistische Gegenwart.*

57. Schillebeeckx, *Die eucharistische Gegenwart,* pp. 97f.

58. At this point the interpretation that Schillebeeckx gives to the history of theology seems to me to be too one-sided, because it is interested only in the relative, historical correctness of the formulations of the Council of Trent and accords no attention to the relative, historical correctness of the counter positions held by the Reformers.

59. The definitive identity of the essence which is expressed in the traditional concept of substance can be given expression in the framework of a historical perspective of reality in its limitless changeability only in terms of the finality of that which results from the processes of change. A change in meaning which remains a merely transitory moment in this flux, since it will be superseded by further changes in meaning, cannot attain a definitive essence. Thus without the concept of an ultimate meaning that results from the process of transformation of meaning there would still remain the old dualism between sign and what it signifies. Only ultimate, eschatological meaning has the definitive truth which the Aristotelian concept of substance implied. Only through the finality of the change in meaning which is involved in the blessing of bread and wine in the Eucharist is the mistrust eliminated which has been aroused by the concept of transignification.

60. By contrast, Schillebeeckx's discussion does not escape a dualism of transubstantiation and transignification. The whole drive of his book *Die eucharistische Gegenwart* (The Eucharistic Presence) is toward a new interpretation of transubstantiation through the concept of transignification, and he deals with the decisive point, that the essence or substance of things precedes our perception (p. 86) and reveals itself only in the transformation of experienced meaning. Yet even so, in contrast to Schoonenberg, he concludes that "the eucharistic transignification is not identical with transubstantiation," even though it "is inwardly connected with it" (p. 101). The differ-

ence and the "metaphysical priority" of transubstantiation, which should already be assumed in transignification (p. 102) is traced back to the distinction between being and appearance. On the other hand, we may suggest that the very difference between being (or essence) and appearance is to be found in the historical process of human experience of meaning and arises from the distinction between the temporary and the final meaning of that which we perceive in our experience, so that the question of essence becomes a theme of eschatology, and final meaning coincides with the essence or being of things and events. Cf. my article "Erscheinung als Ankunft des Zukünftigen," *Studia Philosophica* 26 (1966), pp. 192–207 (E.T., "Appearance as the Arrival of the Future," in my *Theology and the Kingdom of God* [Westminster Press, 1969], pp. 127–143).

61. More properly we might have hoped for the insight that on the basis of genuinely Aristotelian thought consubstantiation is just as nonsensical as transubstantiation, because it violates the axiom *omne ens est unum* (something cannot be itself and at the same time something else as well). Hegel was the first to see this as the truth of the "something" itself, not in the sense of a silent coexistence, but as transition into its opposite. And here we are in reality already on the way toward interpreting transubstantiation as transignification.

62. On this question, see Skibbe, "Das Proprium des Abendmahls."

63. Althaus, *Die christliche Wahrheit*, pp. 587f.

64. "The Unity of the Church and the Unity of Mankind," *Study Encounter* V, 4 (1969), pp. 163–181.

65. Raiser (ed.), *Löwen 1971*.

66. See the comments by E. Lange, "Die ökumenische Utopie, oder: Was bewegt die ökumenische Bewegung? Am Beispiel Löwen 1971," *Menscheneinheit—Kircheneinheit* (1972), pp. 106ff., 126ff., 140f.

67. See the comments of J. Meyendorff in Löwen over the reaction of the Orthodox Churches to the shift from theology to secular anthropology that had been developing since 1963 ("Einheit der Kirche—Einheit der Menschheit," *Ökumenische Rundschau* 21 (1972), pp. 160ff.).

68. E. Schlink, "Die Bedeutung von 'Faith and Order' für die ökumenische Bewegung in Deutschland und die Evangelische Kirche in Deutschland," *Ökumenische Rundschau* 21 (1972), pp. 145ff.

69. *Lumen Gentium* I, art. 5.

70. N. Luhmann ("Religiöse Dogmatik und gesellschaftliche Evolution," in Dahm, Luhmann, and Stoodt, eds., *Religion—System und Sozialisation* [1972], pp. 20ff.) stresses the formation of religion as a social subsystem, in contrast to positions such as those of Malinowski and Durkheim, which identify religion with the society as a whole. But he agrees with the thesis advanced by these authors, and also T.

Luckmann (*Das Problem der Religion in der modernen Gesellschaft* [1963], pp. 34ff.) that the theme of religion is the "universal meaningfulness of human social existence." Cf. Luhmann, p. 22.

71. According to Luhmann, pp. 21, 28ff., the process of such differentiation explains "the historical fate of religion," the transformations in its function for the whole of society. The meaning that contingent historical events such as the Reformation and its political consequences have for the development of modern society can easily be underestimated in such an interpretation.

72. Cf. E. Voegelin, *Die neue Wissenschaft des Politischen* (1959), pp. 81ff.

73. It is not possible here to discuss their indispensable nature for the individual's life, involving, as they do, the psychological problem of identity.